To Matt

With compliments

for all your help with

this.

Adam Samuel

COMPLIANCE

A short book

COMPLIANCE

A short book

Adam Samuel

First published in 2024 by Intellectual Perspective Press

To find out more about our authors and books visit:
www.intellectualperspective.com

CONTENTS

PRAISE FOR "COMPLIANCE – A SHORT BOOK"

Adam's book provides a concise, frank and very useful guide that cuts through the regulatory minefield of compliance. A compelling read for firms both large and small.

Fay Goddard, former CEO of The Personal Finance Society.

Compliance – A Short Book, is a valuable resource for anyone in the field of compliance, from seasoned professionals to those just starting their career. Its concise, no-nonsense style and real-world examples make it an accessible guide to understanding and implementing effective compliance practices.

Marios Sciathas, Chief Executive, European Institute of Management and Finance

Adam provides a unique view of a complex topic. He has an uncanny ability to see through the complicated and plot a pathway through which leaves you with a firm grasp of not only the challenge, but also the solution. These words should sit on the desk of any one with a link to the compliance world and act as a reminder that it should not to be an insular and 'police' like activity, but rather a partner which helps the business to succeed.

Nick West, Head of Learning & Development, Julius Baer UK & Guernsey

Are you contemplating a career in Compliance? Seeking to understand the real challenges and how you might make a difference to the organisations you serve? Or maybe you are a board member finding yourself with responsibility for a function called "Compliance" and are wondering how to manage it for maximum effectiveness?

What does Compliance do? How can it do whatever it does better? What are the traits of a good Compliance person, and what are the mistakes he or she must avoid? And why does this matter?

All these questions and more are explored and, where possible, answered, in Mr Samuel's thoroughly readable book. Mr Samuel is clearly a man who knows whereof he speaks, basing his observations on practical examples of the day-to-day challenges faced by Compliance functions past and present. I enjoyed reading it, even though I have spent a career learning the lessons Mr Samuel explains lucidly and concisely. I recommend this book to anyone whose role involves, or deals with, or is even the customer of, a Compliance function.

Andy Gordon, Temporary Compliance Officer

Compliance is often perceived as being a dusty mixture of tedious and pointless rules designed to accelerate the corrosive nature of bureaucracy. Adam has the unerring ability to bring compliance to the forefront of business acumen and raise it from the impenetrable doldrums of boredom with genuine anecdotes highlighting pitfalls versus success, simply for the want of understanding compliance. Adam's book and his "brand of compliance" may well save your business's life.

Howard Northover, Director and financial adviser, ES Walton & Co.

For many years, I have heard Adam set out his thinking on compliance and regulation, how firms can avoid obvious pitfalls to the benefit of them and their clients. This book distils his thinking. Anyone owning, running or working in a regulated retail financial service business should read this book.

John Lappin, Journalist, former editor of Money Marketing

It was an interesting read and useful insight for those working in compliance. It was written in plain English too which is always helpful! New recruits may find it useful to refer to as part of a structured training programme.

Trudi Mellon, former project manager, Pensions & FSAVC Review,
MGM Assurance and head of exams, the CII.

I don't think there is anyone with a greater understanding or experience of the compliance challenges facing UK regulated (and other) financial institutions than Adam .. or with more sound and practical suggestions on how to address them.

Andrew Hilton, Director, Corporate Training Partnerships Limited (CTP)

PREFACE

This book is the product of over thirty years of financial services compliance-related work in the UK, enlivened by excursions to Hong Kong and Cyprus. Thousands of people have influenced my thinking on this subject. Some would want to remain nameless since they gave me some of the stories and experiences that appear in the examples that I hope bring the text to life. Malachy McClelland and Karyl Nairn in different ways helped me make it over the line with this book: Malachy by his dogged support and comments on the manuscript, and Karyl for suggesting that I use song lyrics to help free up my thoughts about the various topics covered. Sandy Hoyland took the second draft apart with a passion and thoroughness that I have never experienced before and grounded this work in the real compliance world. Daryl Peagram and Mathew Priestley also gave me the benefit of their very different viewpoints on the third draft. Responsibility, though, for the text remains mine.

I have made a conscious effort to make this book short and relatively free of references. If readers want to know where things come from, they should contact me using the details on www.adamsamuel.com.

PART 1: THE BASICS

1

INTRODUCTION

Most organisations need some form of compliance: somebody, perhaps a team or department, dedicated to keeping them in line with what various rules demand they do. In a vast array of fields, books have examined this role in terms of the detailed provisions that entities and individuals have to follow.

This book tries to ask and answer a different question: how is good compliance done in practice? Other questions may lead us to the answer. Are there core features of compliance work and the people that do it? What is the real flavour of the subject?

I have spent over thirty years in and around the financial services sector. As one of the most regulated fields, it provides a useful starting point. Hopefully, though, this book will interest and inspire discussion well beyond the world of banks, investment companies and financial advisers to businesses generally, hospitals, charities and other organisations.

2

WHAT IS COMPLIANCE?

This looks like a much easier question than it is. Compliance is about obeying rules laid down by the law and other authorities. That is, until it is not.

First, the organisation that can claim 100% observance of all rules and regulations is likely to be both dishonest and insolvent. Even the most clear-cut law (do not park on a double-yellow line) is capable of being interpreted differently, depending on the facts (the car may be a tiny bit over the line or the driver may have abandoned the car to save someone's life). There is always a gap between rules and their application to facts.

Authorities often expect organisations to comply not just with the letter but the spirit of their instructions. They do not always draft rules clearly, anticipate or understand how their rules will work in a particular context or act competently.

Compliance often involves interpreting rules and deciding how they apply to the business before trying to ensure that the organisation complies with them. Sometimes, Compliance has to concede that the business will break or not comply fully with certain rules in order to continue to function sensibly.

Some of the biggest calls that Compliance has to make concern whether to tell the business to shut down or not start an activity which itself does not break any rules but which will almost certainly result in widespread non-compliance. The three big consumer financial services compliance issues of the last thirty years (mortgage endowments, people leaving their employer pension schemes or not joining them, and payment protection insurance) all share this feature.

Compliance may involve an effort to be as compliant as possible or practicable.

> A well-known mortgage brokerage wanting to display ten offers from different lenders could not present the lengthy representative example required on the same page without wrecking its website layout. Perhaps, a button saying "click here for a representative example" would not have met the requirements of the rules. Nobody, though, would have suffered since very few people read or understand the examples anyway. The click button instruction would have been nearly compliant.

This often entails an attempt to prioritise the most important things over the minor details.

> A bank's compliance department focused entirely on whether the deadline for acknowledging complaints was one of three possible different times over a 24-hour period. In doing so, it missed the fact that the firm was wrongly rejecting customer grievances and was referring customers to the Ombudsman using obscure and ungrammatical English.

Compliance cannot operate effectively in or by creating a zero-tolerance environment. Humans make mistakes. Fear usually generates more errors than it stops.

Compliance, though, earns its money when it prevents something of fundamental importance. This is not just about instructing the organisation on the existence or meaning of rules. It often involves knowing the organisation and discovering things that are wrong or may cause major rule breaches in the future. Stopping a dangerous surgeon from operating or a company from marketing a defective product saves lives and billions of pounds. In both cases, this requires Compliance to become deeply unpopular by stopping somebody doing something apparently lucrative which could turn into a nightmare for the organisation and its customers. Most of the biggest problems in this area involve somebody or their ideas being indulged when they should not have been.

Sometimes, the nightmare never happens because nobody notices the non-compliance. A badly built house may not collapse, at least not in the builder's lifetime.

> In the early 1990s, a number of businesses recommended interest-only mortgages whose capital was to be repaid using the tax-free cash payable on retirement of typically 25% of the fund built up through the regular investment of pension payments. The financial regulators here never caught up with the irresponsibility of making the payment of a home loan depend on the success of a very long-term pension investment. Intriguingly, firms did suffer here when the customers should have been putting their money into their employers' arrangements instead. A massive proactive review into that aspect of the problem, ordered by regulators, cost the industry billions of pounds. Firms also tended to lose complaint cases at the Ombudsman concerning pension mortgages and ended up paying complainants chunks of their outstanding loans.

Is compliance about enforcing ethical standards within an organisation? Many regulators and courts draw consciously or otherwise from their own notions of morality to fill gaps. A number of professional rulebooks contain vague concepts such as "acting with integrity" and "using due skill, care and diligence" or "prioritising customer needs over the business". The law on integrity and honesty speaks of people with defective "moral compasses". Regulators frequently talk of the need for those they supervise to act ethically. The problem with these exhortations lies in the absence of any precision or definition. Compliance may involve defining morality in terms of usable rules and adding them to what we think of as legal and regulatory requirements.

So, compliance does not involve ensuring that the business complies with the rules. Such an outcome is probably impossible. Anyway, the best people in this field go beyond making decisions about whether something complies to considering whether an activity will probably cause rules to be broken and harm to customers in significant ways. Insight, knowledge and awareness may all be more important in this area than a mastery of the details of the rules themselves.

2.1 What is Compliance supposed to do?

Considering the difficulties of defining compliance, it might be more practical to explain what compliance people or teams are supposed to be doing. This depends enormously on the size and resources of an organisation. Many smaller businesses outsource considerable amounts of their compliance activities, although never responsibility for them. The good ones among them, though, keep a tight grip on activities at the heart of the firm.

The traditional view and a sensible starting point is that Compliance establishes and reviews procedures and policies, advises the organisation and monitors its activities and provides reports to senior management, including the Board, and outside authorities. In these areas, nothing in the organisation can fall outside the compliance function's remit. By the same token, in an organisation of any size, Compliance should not be doing the activities that it monitors. Otherwise, it is "marking its own homework".

In this sense, Compliance forms the second not the first "line of defence" in the organisation's risk management framework. The first line does the job, the second monitors it and the third audits it. So, the person signing off an advertising campaign as meeting the regulatory requirements before it starts sits in the first line, not the second, and, using this purist view, does not perform a compliance function. The same applies to the "compliance" person sitting on the product governance committee considering proposals for new business lines. Somebody else has to monitor the activities of the sign-off or compliance person in these situations to prevent the controls of the organisation being compromised. In a large financial institution, this can be crucial as a way of stopping the front-line compliance person becoming so integrated with the other parts of the business as to be unable to say no when required to do so.

We need two reservations about this. First, a small organisation will lack sufficient staff to provide the second line in the way described. An occasional random external check or an internal or external audit function (traditionally the third line) may have to perform what in a major bank should probably be the second line oversight. Secondly, it seems silly to argue that people whose primary function is to characterise as non-compliant certain proposals are not performing a compliance function. Some of the most effective people in an organisation carry out these first-line roles. An anaesthetist who prevents a surgeon from going into an operating theatre while not in a mentally fit state reduces risk far more than an auditor looking at what went wrong after an overtired doctor made a mess of an operation.

2.2 So what does compliance do in practice?

The rest of this book focuses on the key compliance tasks, many of which are done by the compliance team or people within the organisation. Sometimes Compliance's role is limited to supervising or monitoring what someone else has done. At others, it is expected to take charge.

The first and most important requirement is to ensure that the business meets any operating conditions: authorisation or licensing, having the correct individuals filling particular posts and having their appointments ratified where necessary by outside bodies and holding sufficient capital to keep regulators happy.

Compliance has to set up or at least review the operating procedures and policies of the organisation where they have any impact on the entity's ability to comply with key or fundamental rules. It has to offer practical reasoned advice to the business when it needs help. It has to monitor what the organisation is doing at all stages of its life.

The regulators of the organisation need someone inside it with whom to communicate. Compliance typically performs this role or ensures that somebody else is doing so. This typically involves reporting to the authorities sensitive matters which could be very damaging to individuals and even the body itself.

> A firm received a justified complaint from another business that an individual taken on but not approved to be an adviser was giving regulated advice to her former clients. A quick notification to the regulator of this and a review which failed to identify any customer detriment protected the firm from further investigation.

More mundanely, regulators routinely ask for information about businesses or require regular standard reports.

The Board or governing body of the organisation (typically both) should expect to receive reports from Compliance on the significant issues that it has discovered. At least one EU Directive (that still forms part of UK regulation) insists on the compliance team in financial product manufacturers supplying the Board with information about the products manufactured and sold. Like the rest of the entity, the governing body can and does seek Compliance's advice on how the organisation needs to behave and probably should be monitored by Compliance to ensure the appropriate performance of its duties.

As already mentioned, Compliance-focused individuals, although not necessarily the whole department, may have to participate in and sometimes operate a veto or sign-off of decisions concerning things like financial promotions and product governance. This does not fit neatly within the standard three lines of defence model (line one does it, two monitors it, three audits it). This work is very much first line. However, it seems artificial to deny the compliance content of this extremely important activity.

Compliance has to handle major crises if they have anything to do with the organisation's observance of applicable regulation. This "Houston we have a problem" role frequently brings together all the other functions just described here. A company in serious trouble needs to tell the authorities what has happened and what the firm is doing to fix it. The organisation may need to tighten up its procedures and satisfy the regulator of its keenness to learn from its problem by commissioning a wider review in this area. A good compliance function needs to keep senior management and the Board informed on all this and advise them on how best to handle the situation.

Finally and more generally, Compliance should be the voice of the client within the firm. That sometimes becomes lost otherwise.

We will look at all of these roles in more detail, later in the book. However, before we do so, we need to consider the type of people suitable for a compliance role.

3

WHAT SORT OF PERSON SHOULD DO COMPLIANCE?

Compliance roles require a number of skills, knowledge and personal characteristics that can probably never be found in one person and some of which may conflict with each other. A no doubt imperfect list of the features that every team needs could include:

- High levels of integrity;
- Courage, resilience and steadfastness;
- Quick, reasonable and accurate judgement, including an ability to prioritise;
- Reasonable comfort in having responsibility;
- Curiosity;
- Emotional intelligence and communication skills;
- Credibility, knowledge and the ability to learn;
- The ability to delegate and allocate resources;
- Diversity; and
- "Feel".

3.1 High levels of integrity

High levels of at least professional integrity and a strong moral compass lie at the heart of every good compliance officer. The role can give individuals access to highly sensitive information and considerable amounts of corporate power. Compliance officers, like other employees, have gone to jail for defrauding their employers.

3.2 Courage, resilience and steadfastness

The ability to contradict powerful people lies at the heart of the compliance role. The "no" hammer has to remain in the individual's kitbag, ready to be used at any time. People want Compliance to be positive and constructive and help organisations achieve their objectives. This only works, though, where the department retains the ultimate weapon of just saying "stop it now", to be used when really needed.

Stopping people in this way requires the ability to withstand pressure, often from very powerful people. Courage and steadfastness are essential. Major financial scandals often stem from lines of business which at the time made huge profits for the business. The effect of the subsequent regulatory action and compensation payments not only obliterated those gains, they created huge financial holes in the businesses involved. The compliance people who ignore something in order to maintain a profit flow and to remain on friendly terms with powerful people can ultimately destroy businesses and organisations, and should and sometimes do end up personally accountable for this.

The ability to handle personal unpopularity plays a central role in the ability to make dispassionate correct decisions which may thwart large numbers of people in their personal or organisational goals. A keenness to please may not be consistent with the ability to wield the "no" hammer that is central to all good compliance. Sometimes, compliance becomes too close to the business to make difficult decisions.

> An important financial adviser was discovered to have stolen large sums of money from elderly vulnerable customers to fund a cocaine habit. Staff in the organisation had suspected that the individual had a narcotics issue but had failed to take steps to ensure his strict supervision and the treatment of his problem. When asked about this, the compliance officer said: "oh we just thought that that was James being James." (James is not his real name.) Most of the senior management had known James for many years and were reluctant to intervene and even pick up on some signs that he was not following internal procedures designed to keep files and customers safe.

3.3 Quick, reasonable and accurate judgement, including an ability to prioritise

The ability to judge things quickly and accurately plays a crucial role. Compliance often needs to go beyond the question of whether something is compliant or not to predicting whether, should the company proceed with what it plans to do, it will end up doing significant regulatory damage. There is a considerable element of prediction involved.

Good judgement often involves prioritising accurately and responding proportionately to different issues. Some people confuse decisiveness over minor matters with good judgement. It is almost always far more important to stop a dangerous financial adviser from making unsuitable recommendations or stealing from clients than to file a regulatory return accurately or on time.

Speed, does not always equate to quality. Good judgement may involve working with existing personnel to raise standards gradually, rather than the all-too-common and highly disruptive snap corporate response of a departmental reorganisation.

3.4 Reasonable comfort in having responsibility

The ability to make good quick judgements and withstand pressure may reflect the compliance person's reasonable level of comfort in bearing responsibility for making big decisions. Organisations need people doing this type of work to be anxious and concerned about it and its impact on the firm, its consumers and individual employees. There is, though, a fine line between this and indecision. A tendency to avoid taking responsibility for big decisions, particularly where the business has the same issue or is heading in the wrong direction, exposes the organisation to potential failure.

3.5 Curiosity

Compliance needs to be nosey. Much of its task involves finding things going on that nobody wants it to discover. That requires a combination of curiosity and know-how to locate information.

3.6 Emotional intelligence and communication skills

Compliance should want to work with the business to increase both of their effectiveness. The team needs the organisation to tell them things early so that it can identify key problems and their solution well in advance. It also has to persuade the business to follow its advice.

While it has to be able to handle unpopularity, Compliance needs social and communication skills in order to achieve these things. It also has to display sensitivity to the people it oversees or monitors. Some of the role entails being the person to whom people turn when they are troubled. Listening skills and empathy earn respect and achieve persuasion. They also enable the team to receive material that can be crucial to its monitoring work. That also requires discretion. People will not confide about a department problem if Compliance is going to leak their identity to their bosses. Like a good journalist, Compliance has to protect its sources. Anything that creates a barrier between Compliance and the rest of the organisation reduces the former's persuasiveness and access to information. Bully compliance officers have a limited lifespan.

3.7 Credibility, knowledge and the ability to learn

Compliance people need the respect of those they are trying to influence. Unfairly, personal presentation has an impact.

> In one example, the relevant manager was a man known to have worked in a well-known nightclub which many, particularly female advisers, found distasteful. He made a major contribution to establishing sound procedures and a stronger compliance culture. However, his generally sound advice and guidance was not taken as seriously as it should have been primarily because of his past. His successor, a woman from the financial services industry, had a much more positive impact while conveying the same messages.
>
> In a different company, an adviser told me that the compliance officer was "awesome" which strikes about the right note of fear and respect.

In other cases, knowledge and the ability to do the job generates the required reverence. At a basic level, compliance people have to understand, interpret and apply rules to often complex facts. They then need to be able to translate all this into ordinary language. Alongside communication skills, this involves having an underlying knowledge of both the relevant provisions and the context in which the business operates. To do all this, people need the ability to learn and ask.

> The "awesome" compliance officer commissioned and actively participated in external training sessions on giving investment advice in accordance with the rules. Sitting on the sidelines would have suggested that the regulator's rulebook did not apply to her or that she knew it all.

Compliance people need to explain their opinions clearly, when necessary, with appropriate references. Work experience in the relevant area can build invaluable practical knowledge and credibility so long as it does not create affiliations that distort judgement.

Qualifications do not prove knowledge. However, they represent a commitment to learning and inquiring which carries some weight. In the UK, we rightly insist on investment and mortgage advisers holding qualifications. Compliance people without equivalent exam passes will or perhaps should always struggle to persuade people that they know better. Currently, there are no minimum requirements in this area. However, a "professional" needs the credibility of relevant certifications. For all that they test the ability to do exams, this type of assessment mirrors quite well the environment in which compliance people have to make quick "on-the-hoof" decisions. The process of studying for tests in this way helps to instil that indefinable sense of "feel" that, as we will see, is something of a job requirement.

3.8 The ability to delegate and allocate resources

Few if any compliance departments can do all the jobs expected of it effectively without external help. Often, in large organisations, crucial legal opinions on whether certain activities fall inside the scope of a particular authority's ambit come from a specialist department or outside counsel. Compliance then has to be able to apply the advice received in the actual context.

After the collapse of Lehman Brothers in 2008 led to the failure of numerous structured investment products, a bank that distributed them argued to the UK regulator that if the marketing material had mentioned the investment bank's name, it would have been necessary to issue a prospectus. The Financial Services Authority responded correctly that if that was the case, either a prospectus should have been issued or the firm should not have marketed the product. External legal advice could have told the bank this before it sold the investments.

When difficult legal issues arise, Compliance has to add its judgement to the technical advice that it has received. This often means blocking the marketing of the product.

Santander was fined for a promotion that was not clear about the extent to which its product was covered by the Financial Services Compensation Scheme. The correct answer depended on which component part of the product failed (none ultimately did). This was far too complicated for the firm to communicate safely to their customers. In the circumstances, Compliance should have stopped the bank selling what was a perfectly legal offering.

Compliance people have to know their limitations and be able to delegate tasks to other parts of the business. Much of their work involves form filling. Some people have those skills and others do not. Tying up a big picture compliance person with answering a pointless regulatory questionnaire does not constitute an efficient use of resources.

3.9 Diversity

Teams that all come from the same background struggle to pick up things that lie outside their experience and cultural knowledge. They also tend to support people with whom they feel comfortable – often people like them. Compliance needs detachment from as well as involvement in the organisation. Also, different perspectives within the team prevent complacency and develop insights into both the inside of the organisation, its corporate culture and leadership and the world beyond it.

> When social media was developing, a lack of interest in or technical knowledge of the different types of communication could make it difficult to monitor their use by staff. It is impossible to monitor Snapchat use without knowing that the images fade almost as soon as they are sent!

Compliance's range of influence extends so far that a broad general knowledge (and the consequent awareness of its gaps) can play as great a role as a detailed recall of the rule book. A good example is article 1(3) of the Advertising Standards Authority's Non-Broadcast Code:

"Marketing communications must be prepared with a sense of responsibility to consumers and to society."

Unless you know about society's issues with debt and alcohol, you may not realise how easily an advert seeming to promote either could fall foul of this. (Knowledge of various religions' attitudes to alcohol should probably steer you away from associating that with your product anyway.)

3.10 "Feel"

The final feature of the perfect compliance person or team is the totally indefinable sense of "feel". One could call it judgement but that suggests a weighing of arguments and application of rules. "Feel" is the sense that tells Compliance that certain things are unacceptable, typically if they aim to circumvent rules introduced for good reasons. The same notion might affect the way in which the firm deals with its regulator. It might take the calculated risk of telling the Authority that it is trying its best to comply with a rule that is unworkable in a particular context, engaging with the regulator about it and perhaps applying for a waiver from the offending provision. More commonly, this sense of "touch" leads a firm to disclose things to the regulator, knowing that the authority is not interested in them, in order to put down a marker in the event of a subsequent investigation. One might respond to a major internal compliance problem by telling the regulator of a planned external review of the procedures, knowing that this is much cheaper for the regulator than enforcement action.

When dealing with authorities, one often has to decide when to challenge the authority and when to try to make it easy for it. Officials may not realise that some of their less important demands on businesses waste vast amounts of small firms' compliance resources. That is unless somebody, perhaps an external compliance consultant, tells them this on behalf of a regulated business. Few want to expose themselves to the risk of being seen to be awkward by a powerful public body. So, they mention the problem to people that the Financial Conduct Authority (FCA) does not regulate but who know people there.

> Some years ago, a financial adviser took one compliance person's advice, against the many voices he heard to the contrary, and accepted a request from the regulator to give evidence in an Upper Tribunal (court) case. It is very difficult (although not impossible) for the authority to accuse its own past witness of acting badly.

Perfect compliance people do not exist. If they did, they would have to be brave enough to stand up to you, persuasive enough to influence you and knowledgeable enough to tell you what you need to know and then do roughly the same to the regulator while all along having the feel of a good poker player!

We will now look at the various jobs that compliance people do.

PART 2: THE TASKS

4

ENSURING THAT THE CONDITIONS OF TRADING ARE MET

Organisations need to meet particular requirements for starting off or continuing in a particular area of activity: capital adequacy, specific infrastructure, authorisations and registrations with public authorities and the like. Compliance needs to know the pre-conditions for operating in the way intended. It will be expected to intervene swiftly to stop the organisation doing anything if it has failed to obtain the necessary permissions. Compliance will also be expected to ensure that the operations continue to meet these requirements throughout the business' life.

For this, the team needs to know all the activities, client types and locations involved in the business and the various bodies that may have an interest in regulating or supervising it. Obtaining a respectable legal opinion on whether an activity falls within a particular authority's ambit is often the smart way to protect the organisation from operating without the right licenses.

A major bank had clients in various Caribbean islands and asked its new international compliance manager to discover whether it needed banking licenses in those countries to continue to provide the services concerned. It was shocking to discover that nobody had ever asked the question. The new manager, though, just had to assemble a list of the bank's offerings and the location and type of its customers in the region and obtain opinions from lawyers in the relevant islands and then check with the UK authorities that it had no problem with these activities.

A number of organisations either do not ask these questions of their lawyers or fail to communicate the answers to staff on the ground. This creates problems when a regulator catches up with the company. Compliance also needs to translate the opinion that it has received into clear guidance as to which activities and products are regulated by a particular authority and which are not.

Some regulators provide considerable assistance with both applications for authorisations and then subsequent changes to the relevant "permissions". Even then, a firm will have to identify relevant regulators and complete any necessary forms and sometimes provide a business plan. Here some outsourcing can reduce the burden considerably. Companies exist to take these tasks off the business's hands to everyone's advantage including the regulators'.

> For example, every website of a firm regulated by the Financial Conduct Authority (FCA) has to say that it is regulated by that authority. However, it is both misleading and a breach of that authority's rules not to amend the website footer to indicate that the FCA does not regulate a particular activity when discussing it, such as commercial buy-to-let mortgages. If nobody involved in either the design or sign-off of a website knows which activities fall outside the regulator's ambit or tells the website design people, mistakes will inevitably occur.

Firms need to complete and file necessary applications for the authorisation and regulatory approval of senior individuals. Typically, Compliance either does this job or oversees it. Often, smaller organisations sensibly outsource this to people with relevant experience. Compliance has to check the forms on the way out and ensure that they are both accurate and have been safely sent to the right bodies. Most problems in this area stem from either false details on the application form or a failure to respond to regulators' queries. Compliance needs to address both problems, making any necessary corrections as quickly as possible. An inability to reply quickly to correspondence leads authorities to conclude reasonably that the firm cannot safely operate in a regulated environment or requires higher levels of scrutiny.

Although financial management sits firmly with the finance director or its equivalent, Compliance has to know that the organisation meets any capital adequacy or similar requirements. The difficulty here is that the executives just mentioned are primarily responsible for accounts and all too frequently fail to share key information with other Board members let alone the compliance department. Most if not all staff in a compliance function will typically lack the technical competence to check accounts and provisioning and can end up feeling hoodwinked by the combination of a powerful finance director and an inadequate audit committee. Insisting on proper independent auditing and offering any help in the process of assessing capital adequacy may be all that can be done.

In an accounting scandal case, one of the big four accounting firms gave a clean audit to the accounts. It was little comfort to Compliance to learn that the Financial Reporting Council subsequently fined the auditors for its inadequate work.

What can Compliance be expected to do here? Much depends on what the team knows or can ferret out. Ideally, Compliance should know and understand the business, build relationships across the firm and engender a culture or atmosphere of openness and integrity. However, where management decides to conceal information, Compliance can be on something of "a hiding to nothing". The only thing one can expect is for the latter to read the annual report and raise concerns where it does not match its hands-on experience.

The Annual Report asserted that "our credit quality is excellent" and "we sell optional payment protection insurance". Compliance and others within the organisation know (ideally the product governance and marketing people) that the firm seems to lend to everyone and if customers do not buy the insurance, they are told to expect a negative response to their loan applications. Compliance and the other staff aware of this must state their objections at least internally and tell the regulator if nothing is done to correct the statement concerned. Where the company has a formal stock exchange listing, misleading the markets in this way breaches the UK Listing Rules and can amount to Securities Fraud in Britain and elsewhere.

Compliance must not collude with decisions to "roll-over" non-performing debt, as happened in the accounting scandal just mentioned, to give the misleading impression that arrears do not exist when they clearly do. An ethical sense check from compliance could root out some of the standard scandals in this area.

These cases pose difficult issues for compliance teams. Their reports will almost certainly be ignored. However, the department needs to present these reports first to the Board and then, if the matter is serious enough, to the regulator. Otherwise, when things go wrong, the individuals within it will be accountable for having gone along with senior management.

> In the Equitable Life case, where a promise to apply a minimum guaranteed annuity rate (GAR) to certain policy funds rendered the business moribund, the GAR issue was obvious from the insurers' contracts with its customers. The fact that an internal whistleblower had expressed concerns to the Chief Executive, not the compliance officer, probably made no difference. The difficulty here is that the executive knew of the problem and received conflicting advice on the legality of what he was doing. Compliance should probably have written a report on this but in doing so would only have appeared to duplicate the organisation's external advice and be a futile exercise in self-preservation.

Regulators insist that certain employees or office holders have particular qualifications before they can perform particular functions. Since the mid-1990s, unsupervised financial advisers in the UK have had to pass certain exams. Authorities in other fields insist on large swathes of staff doing continuing professional development (CPD) on top of the examination passes that allow the individuals concerned to do their jobs. Compliance has to at least monitor if not ensure that everyone who needs particular qualifications, Statements of Professional Standing and evidence of CPD has them. Random checks with the professional bodies that administer exams and issue relevant Statements make sense, particularly when concerns arise.

The medical literature contains studies of the role of bogus doctors in medical disasters.[1] Some basic checking of qualifications could avoid many of these incidents.

Organisations often need identified holders of particular positions. The appointment of senior managers, such as the Chief Executive, will often have to be approved by a regulator (a compulsory financial services requirement). Preparing the applications and checking their accuracy can prove to be a key compliance function. Again, one encounters too often fake qualifications or experience on people's CVs which suggests integrity issues. In some cases, details on the form lead to the need for further questioning about a candidate's suitability.

> In one case, the application for approval as a financial adviser revealed an earlier personal bankruptcy without mentioning the insolvency of his companies, improbable projections about future revenues and inconsistent or inaccurate answers to the questions on the form. Each piece of information in itself should have led to further questioning before the firm submitted the form. It could have prevented a later major investment advice scandal.

Sometimes, Compliance's role is just to make sure that the key roles, such as the money laundering reporting officer, have been filled suitably. The next step will be to train the company officers on the implications of their duties.

In one organisation, the CEO did this. He emphasised the importance of the Board not being split. This may have discouraged some directors from challenging his authority (notwithstanding their legal responsibilities in this respect) for fear of not having the rest of the committee's support. In a regulated financial services environment, Compliance should ensure that all staff receive training but not from the CEO on their individual duties both to the company and the relevant regulators and the rulebooks involved.

> A particularly tricky problem for the compliance officer is handling the situation where somebody not on the Board appears to be running the organisation. These shadow directors need to be authorised as actual ones or risk regulatory action against both the individuals concerned and the company. Nominal CEOs do not usually appreciate being told that they have a shadow CEO who is really doing the job! Compliance needs to warn in writing all the relevant parties where someone outside the executive and Board could be controlling the operation.

1. Nocera & Newton, "Bogus Doctor Deceptions during Multi-Casualty Events and Disasters", 15 Prehospital and Disaster Medicine, 3, 25 (2000)

5

SETTING UP THE POLICIES AND PROCEDURES

5.1 The task

Traditionally, Compliance holds the responsibility for the creation, maintenance and ongoing review of policies and procedures. Other parts of the business can write their own procedures. It often works better if they do because they probably know more than Compliance about how the department should operate. This, though, may be a matter of scale. In larger organisations, Compliance usually owns key policies and procedures on subjects such as conflicts of interest, risk frameworks and the like while overseeing and advising on standards and procedures more commonly adopted by the particular business area. Whatever approach the organisation uses, the procedures that it adopts have to be a good fit for the size and scope of, and resources available to, the business.

The terms "policy" and "procedures" can often be used interchangeably. In practice, policies lay down the broad vision behind the procedures. Processes detail what must, may and cannot be done. A policy can introduce procedures. It may also perform other functions.

> In EU and UK financial services complaint handling, businesses have to disclose and typically do so, using their website, how customers should complain and give a broad idea of how cases will be handled including the availability of the Financial Ombudsman Service. The policy may and probably should contain all that information. It can be put on the firm's website and terms and conditions and supplied with acknowledgements of complaints or on request, as the rules require.

All procedures have to fit the organisation, the scope of its activities, its attitudes and the rules that apply to it. A "one-size-fits-all" or in practice "nobody" approach can be lethal. There is nothing worse than a procedure that discusses products and services that the organisation does not offer and rules that do not apply to it. It is difficult enough to persuade people to read these documents. Extra length and irrelevant details do not help and only invite the regulator to ask more intrusive questions and to disregard the useful material actually found in the procedures.

Having said that, starting from scratch every time one drafts anything wastes absurd amounts of time. So, using "one I prepared earlier" for a similar organisation makes sense so long as the person drafting it remains aware of the potential differences and can adapt the document accordingly.

5.2 What needs to be the subject of a process?

Which aspects of the business require procedures depends on the nature of the organisation and its regulatory environment. Authorities often insist on there being particular documented processes, notably for complaint handling or product governance. After that, the business needs to identify its major risk areas and determine which of them would benefit from a written document outlining how things should be done or not.

In practice, one usually looks for the organisation's core activities and design processes to cover them. For example, for a business trying to sell things, one typically finds a procedure to cover promotional activities, dos, don'ts and sign-off processes. The launch of any major campaign without a clearly defined set of rules to follow and an internal check would generate major issues with regulators. This would become worse if they found a breach of "clear, fair and not misleading" or one of the other complex marketing rules that cover various sectors.

The 21st century has seen the emergence of processes for launching or reviewing products and services in financial services markets. Major providers of financial products to consumers have long needed something like this.

> In 1942, the Beveridge Report proposed the nationalisation of industrial assurance, a form of life assurance savings collected door-to-door which only disappeared in the early 1990s for reasons of cost. The report noted:[1] "The high proportion of the premiums paid by the poorest classes that became absorbed in the expenses and profits of Industrial assurance has been the subject of adverse comment by every independent body that has investigated the subject, from the Royal Commission on Friendly Societies which reported in 1874 to the Cohen Committee which reported in 1933."

Compliance has to design or oversee the construction of procedures in order to meet the demands of a number of EU Directives on investments and insurance and, in the UK, a variety of provisions requiring products and services to offer value for money. The same department also needs to review regularly these relatively formal processes for adopting, testing, marketing and reviewing products. This requires Compliance to know the company's products and services, how they work, the ways in which the organisation distributes them, how things can go wrong and what happens when they do.

Often, disasters within the organisation lead to the discovery of a risk and a need to determine how this should be handled.

> After a compliance problem emerged in a financial firm, it commissioned a rewriting of its sales and advice procedures. Perhaps because the business did not train staff properly in relation to the changes or monitor their adoption adequately, issues continued to arise which the new document should have resolved easily. The more effective move was to centralise the way in which "paraplanning", (the research and preparation required for the giving of advice) was done. That enabled Compliance to discover more easily about advisers not following compliance procedures.

While an external review of processes after a major problem has emerged often keeps regulators happy (it is much cheaper for it than taking enforcement action against the firm), the danger exists that these re-writings merely supply words to the organisation, rather than anything of substance. They may also create "monster documents" covering everything that went wrong during the crisis which, by obscuring the procedures' key focus and intention, achieve nothing.

My first and happily only experience of employee theft driven by a narcotics addiction led to the insertion of a policy and procedure to cover that subject in every subsequent risk management process I have ever drafted.

This raises a bigger question of whether Compliance should be laying down procedures and policies in areas that typically human resources departments cover. We have seen how personal issues can increase the risk of the company breaking regulatory rules as well as generating employment law concerns. Allegations made by both customers and staff members about individuals' behaviour may supply important warnings about things that may have or are about to go wrong, quite generally. Compliance needs to participate in the development of human resources policies to check for compliance with rules about whistleblowing, at the very least. Waiting to review processes seems too late. It also creates a risk that a perfectly drafted process does not correspond to reality.

> Over the years, a number of hospital scandals have involved healthcare professionals who were not safe to do what they were doing, for any number of reasons. In some of these instances, another doctor or nurse expressed concerns well in advance of the matter coming to light. A compliance function, rather than the chief executive, would have been the perfect team to receive these complaints, force the removal of the individual from the relevant activity and launch further investigations by the police and disciplinary bodies.

One element of office procedures must cover the transmission of information from Human Resources to Compliance. Awareness that an individual is struggling with personal or financial problems can have an impact on the performance of highly sensitive activities. In the interests of transparency, relevant staff need to know this and should be encouraged to tell Compliance when problems of all types appear in the organisation. The team has a difficult balancing act here. It needs a culture of handling private matters in that way so as to encourage appropriate sharing of information. Nevertheless, steps will sometimes have to be taken to protect the organisation, staff and the public which will make it obvious what has happened.

In any event, the organisation's procedures must cover the interaction between Human Resources or personnel departments and other managers whose primary concern should be staff safety and well-being and Compliance. The latter's viewpoint traditionally focuses more on the public and regulators. The limits of each function here have to be clearly delineated alongside the ways in which they need to co-operate.

The frontiers of Compliance's role in either drafting or overseeing procedures can create genuine friction with HR. That department should have its own rules about how to do things, often driven by legal advice. In practice, a compliance function should examine the HR procedures if they exist (and insist on them being written if they do not), check them for obvious problems, make suggestions based on past experience, ensure that an employment lawyer has signed them off and then insist on any adjustments necessary to meet any otherwise unmet requirements of a particular regulator.

Human Resources will have procedures for handling complaints against individuals which involve giving that person a right to respond and a proper hearing. However, the timescales for this may not be consistent with those for handling regulated complaints against the organisation. Upheld complaints against an individual in the latter context may have to be reported to the regulator and referred to in a reference. It may be necessary to separate the HR and complaints aspects of each case. Compliance can then supply references and communicate to regulators information explaining the material supplied. This should make it clear whether the individual concerned was in any sense culpable for what happened.

A similar approach applies to health and safety at work issues. When the Covid pandemic started, some organisations were slow to close down their offices, due to managers' concerns about the control they were about to lose over their staff. In some cases, this broke the law and put staff at risk. As in an industrial or construction environment, Compliance or a similar part of the business should have had processes to ensure staff safety.

Financial services rulebooks have provisions requiring systems and controls to ensure continuity of service to customers. Some of this work could fall within the risk management sections of large companies. At least, Compliance must lay down the requirement to have and regularly test these processes. Detailed involvement here can challenge the limits of Compliance's competence. The repeated shutdowns of cashpoint machines and credit card facilities have at their root complex IT issues. Compliance can insist on independent quality assurance, testing and operational resiliency plans but remains very much at the mercy of the technology side of the business.

5.3 Writing procedures

5.3.1 The skill set

Writing procedures requires particular drafting skills which, firms might do well to appreciate, not all staff have. Clarity of expression, the ability to write in plain but meaningful language and organise thoughts coherently all play a crucial role. Where organisations want to make their processes more accessible through visual presentations, they sometimes need to pair up people who can draft with more visually-talented individuals.

5.3.2 Defining the scope

Unless it is obvious, all processes should begin by indicating their scope: the activity, location and subject-matter concerned at least. Operations in different countries or sectors typically have to follow dissimilar regimes for things. The reader of the procedure must know immediately whether the document applies to the situation that they are facing.

Some parent companies have demonstrated an irritating and dangerous habit of imposing their own countries' processes and promotional material on the rest of the group, not realising or perhaps even caring that the application of different rules or regulatory approaches to the same situation could create compliance nightmares.

The issues could just be cultural. An advert from certain parts of central and eastern Europe involving alcohol may not be seen as antisocial or offensive in a way that it would be in Britain or Tunisia. Some countries' regulators focus more carefully and use their enforcement powers more effectively in particular areas, perhaps where a previous embarrassing scandal has occurred.

The UK regulates promotions for commercial buy-to-let mortgages, residential homeloans and car loans utterly differently, leaving the first to the Advertising Standards Authority (ASA) and subjecting the second and third to both the ASA Codes and two completely different Financial Conduct Authority (FCA) rulebooks. Separate procedures for each type of advert or different sections of a single process devoted to the specific features of the three products and their applicable regimes make obvious sense. A rulebook designed to be applied across Europe would have to be checked against the standards laid down by both ASA and the FCA before the company can adopt it for UK business.

A common danger for large organisations is the development of processes that duplicate resource and overlap. Compliance cannot just draft processes and hope that somebody follows them intelligently across a series of different corporate structures. The procedure has to identify exactly who or which department does what in any given situation. Consequently, people drawing up a cross-group process in a big entity have to know the structure in great detail in order to indicate accurately who in the different parts of the business should be doing what.

> Funds are typically set up as individual companies. Within a corporate group, having separate governance committees for each would cause chaos and be impossible to monitor. This illustrates the importance of adapting processes to the environment in which the organisation operates. A single or small group of processes covering the whole group would ensure that its offering to the public and distribution makes sense, lacks duplication and can be governed properly.

5.3.3 The basis of the procedure

Alongside a description of what the process covers and excludes, the procedure's author should probably add the rules, laws and the like on which the document is based. It is much easier for an organisation to maintain and improve its procedures if it knows the underlying material. When that changes, Compliance needs to review the procedure to ensure that the alterations have been incorporated where necessary.

Generally compliance standards rise when front-line people know and feel comfortable interpreting the rules. They have experienced the ways in which the regulations interact with real life and can easily propose practical and compliant changes to the processes where following them is either unnecessary, difficult or sometimes impossible. Well-drafted procedures, supported by appropriate training, which encourage the readers to look at the underlying rules can also raise educational standards amongst affected staff.

5.3.4 The writing process

Procedures do not drive change; people do. Often a short message works better than ten paragraphs of elegantly drafted text.

The procedures should take the form of an exchange between Compliance and the people doing the job. Compliance can always veto a proposed change where it would probably cause the organisation to breach its legal or other requirements. However, practitioner input may be vital in the initial drafting, and afterwards to bring the document to life and ensure that it addresses the issues that really arise. A great deal of compliance work involves helping teams to make the small changes that turn a likely rule breach into something acceptable. Here, if the department concerned wants to do something, the procedure has to indicate how it can be done acceptably and warn the team about where its risks lie.

The procedure's author can be tempted to repeat what the relevant regulator has said, perhaps with a commentary. That serves no purpose. Users would be better off reading the rules in the original and, as a result, learning how the various provisions fit together. Compliance's job is to translate the rules into something that the staff can understand and implement. Procedures should describe how the organisation goes about doing things in ways that comply. This will typically contain a series of dos and don'ts and desirable and undesirable behaviours which refer to issues within the business. Procedures should never deal with activities in which the business is not engaged except when prohibiting the behaviour concerned.

> Some organisations limit the use of social media in order to be able to control the content that is issued on their behalf. Procedures should not discuss what should or should not be done in a media that is banned by the firm. They should just explain that people should not communicate in the relevant way.

Without becoming too unwieldy, procedures have to cover what the organisation expects of its staff in particular situations and the seriousness with which certain behaviour will be treated. They also need to highlight areas where the organisation has shown ignorance or gone wrong in the past. Presenting details of prior misdemeanours can be left to training! Processes also have to differentiate between wholly unacceptable behaviour and less desirable or optional responses to certain situations.

> The presence of the narcotics policy in a staff manual identifies the problem as one that the organisation takes seriously. This signals the organisation's values as caring about customer safety in the first instance and then about that of other employees and any individual with that type of problem.

Presentation depends a great deal on the audience. Images and real examples help to bring the document to life. However, less spatially aware individuals can find flow charts and other diagrams more unhelpful than a pile of words. A balance, rather than alternative versions of the same document (with their version control issues), can solve this problem.

5.3.5 Ordering the document

In an ideal world, procedures would tackle the most important issues first and then everything else in order of significance. Employees find it difficult to plough through vast amounts of verbiage even with a good index.

In many cases, though, one needs to follow some form of chronological order so that people can follow the intended sequences of behaviour. It may, nevertheless, be useful to begin the procedure by highlighting the major causes of problems. After that, dealing with the issues in the way they actually arise makes more sense.

> The vast majority of enforcement activity in the area of complaints relates to decisions which wrongly reject complaints and inadequate investigations. Procedures should note this briefly at the start. However, one of the classic reasons why cases go out of control in this area is because the firm has not followed the order in which cases should be dealt with. To make any sense, a complaints procedure needs to tackle the issues in the correct order: advance disclosure of how to complain, identification and definition of complaints, acknowledgement, investigation, assessment and response.

Procedures can become lifeless if they become more like a textbook on how to do something. They need to highlight key things that people may not know or appreciate, or find difficult. As documents, they should be guiding readers to take appropriate steps and reject less helpful options. There is something to be said for supplying a commentary to the procedures which the individual can select when keen to learn more about something.

5.4 Implementing the procedures

However well drafted, a procedure cannot achieve anything without training being delivered to ensure that staff understand and follow the document. Those affected must appreciate how it works in practice. The organisation also has to know that staff can implement it. Before adopting the procedures or significant alterations to them, the company should organise interactive discussions or training sessions involving both the people affected by the changes and those responsible for introducing them. This can lead to sensible compliant alterations based on what people on the ground indicate (through their knowledge or otherwise) needs to be covered or handled differently and what does not.

> As an external compliance trainer, I always asks to see any relevant internal procedures before the course. Training should refer to them. An external provider can also discreetly suggest changes that might be needed, prior to the session. In that situation, staff can be told that the procedure is under review (that should always be the case) and that the course forms part of that process.

In an ideal world, the rolling out of a process, however well researched in advance, should highlight its weaknesses. Invited by Compliance to comment, stakeholders should be able to identify features of the draft that fail to reflect the reality of the business or its practical constraints. Compliance can make pre-launch changes.

Things rarely work like this. Sometimes, a new compliance officer arrives to find that no written procedures exist where there should definitely be something. A poor ill-adapted product, perhaps taken from another similar company and quickly amended represents something; a good deal better than nothing, particularly if the regulator asks for a copy. The organisation can supply it with a note truthfully indicating that the organisation is currently reviewing the document.

More commonly, key people when asked to comment on a draft may give the matter less than their full attention. Until implementation, nobody knows how something will work in practice, which aspects people know instinctively and where precise instruction may be needed. In that sense, the procedure review begins at launch, a point that all people affected should appreciate. Everyone needs to be encouraged to add their insight (anonymously if necessary) on how the new document works, and how it helps or hinders the achievement of the desired outcomes.

5.5 Reviews

Every procedure needs a formal review schedule while the organisation must keep the option of altering it to meet both external and internal developments. Any changes need to follow processes designed to maintain both good governance and accurate version control.

A formal review process, after a given length of time, needs to contain several elements. First, the reviewer has to consider whether the document needs altering to reflect developments or foreseeable changes in regulation or the company's products or activities since it was drafted. Secondly, does the procedure reflect what the organisation is or should be doing in practice? Thirdly, can its content and presentation be improved?

The second job can be the most challenging. Much good work happens during procedural reviews when people doing the job explain how they think things could be done more efficiently or comfortably and everyone realises that no reason exists why the organisation should not adopt that approach. User feedback can help determine whether the procedures are emphasising the central points, and could result in some items being relegated to a commentary or notes section.

When one invites stakeholders to comment, there is the risk of a "compliance competition" where everyone tries to demonstrate how much of the rulebook they know. So long as the person running the review can sort the important from the less significant and can thank everyone for their contribution, this should not cause significant issues. New insights may not end up being reflected in the amended process, but could contribute to the organisation's and Compliance's general understanding or be added to the commentary on the process. This emphasises the need to have one person and not a group taking charge of the review. Otherwise, every possible insight on the subject can clog the process.

Compliance needs to understand problems faced by teams in following their "instructions". Pressures, incentives, lack of resources, the impracticality of the requirement or just a lack of general engagement could lie at the heart of the problem. The procedures reviewer needs to work with the people involved to discover the issue, find a solution and reflect it in an amended document.

Finally, one can always improve the writing and presentation of the procedures. Implementation will flag up the areas of greatest importance and perhaps reveal things that can be omitted or relegated to a commentary. Team members with visual flair can produce more animated presentations that come closer to catching the readers' imagination. The correction of typographical and grammatical errors and improved layout always increase a document's credibility.

---

1. Appendix D, paragraph 35

6

COMPLIANCE ADVICE TO THE ORGANISATION

6.1 How it works

Compliance's advice function operates in a variety of ways. First, people reasonably want to know what rules apply in certain situations and how to find those provisions. A general open request for guidance in dealing with certain types of situation will probably require a more detailed analysis, showing how key materials (with links to where they can be found) apply to the problem described. Here, Compliance not only wants to resolve the issue, it wants to make the whole subject easier and more accessible. A more knowledgeable and compliant workforce can leave the Compliance department to deal with more weighty problems and reduce the latter's subsequent monitoring workload. For this reason alone, Compliance should encourage the business to ask it for advice.

Compliance should always welcome both these types of enquiry and respond quickly to them. It should explain that there is no such thing as a "silly question". Anyone who phrases an enquiry in those terms demonstrates their concern about the subject. Besides, plenty of commonly accepted views on how to behave turn out to be completely wrong. "Emperor's new clothing" questions can reveal a layer of misconceptions that the organisation may have built up over considerable amounts of time.

Encouraging people to engage with regulatory issues should be part of the department's agenda. Follow-up comments from the questioner can valuably expose a weakness in the analysis supplied or suggest a different way of looking at the issue. This open interaction brings compliance much closer to the business, earns it respect and makes it much easier for everyone to make progress, including the person answering the question. After all, the act of doing the necessary research may expand the knowledge of the respondent as much as anyone else's.

The advice function feeds into other areas of Compliance's activities. Questions asked can reveal areas of risk or weakness which need monitoring more carefully. The insight generated from what should usually be friendly exchanges between departments enables procedures to focus where they most need to. Indeed, an answer can lead to an amendment to the relevant procedures or a commentary on them to ensure that all relevant personnel know about the matter. The department can publish its opinions in full or in summary for people to study and hopefully apply. This may continue the process of the business taking compliance issues seriously and helping Compliance to understand how the organisation really works.

6.2 How to answer requests for advice

The compliance advice function can, though, prove to be one of the more dangerous and complicated jobs. All too often, people ask for help in this area, not because they really want to know the correct answer, but to receive a "blessing" for what they propose to do. Consequently, questions can be put in ways designed to generate a particular reply.

> I was asked whether it was possible to create a compliant single premium payment protection insurance policy. The answer is technically yes. The response said that but added that the product as currently designed could not be provided to customers without breaking the regulator's Principle 6 (treating customers fairly) and explained why. Industry provisions for badly sold insurance of this type have been estimated at about £50 billion.

Compliance can generate major regulatory issues by sticking to the precise question posed and being misinterpreted as approving unacceptable behaviour in a different area. The correct response is to seek more information about the context of the inquiry, the problem that the questioner is trying to solve and then to answer both what was and what should have been asked.

Opinions, as opposed to responses to requests for simple "information dumps", need to follow a structure with which everyone who interacts with Compliance is familiar and which Compliance can defend if something goes wrong in years to come. (Strangely, it should resemble the response to a customer complaint.)

- Thank you;
- The question put and how the respondent understands it;
- Any other questions that the opinion is going to answer;
- The facts;
- The view or conclusion on each of the two sets of questions, supported by references, links to relevant rules or guidance and ideally the internal procedures;
- Any necessary concluding comments or suggestions of next steps to be taken.

Usually opinions have to be based on underlying facts which the respondent needs to assemble by carrying out further enquiries or independent research. There is something to be said for refusing to answer hypothetical questions in this area. Even if the underlying facts can be stated briefly, they should still be there to ensure that nobody interprets the opinion as applying to something different or approving behaviour of which the person giving the advice is unaware.

References to published material (laws, rules and commentary) play an important role here because the opinion seeks not just to answer the question but to enable recipients to develop their own knowledge and insight. The description of any next steps can prove useful for both sides of the exchange.

A crucial aspect of compliance work is the replacement of unacceptable or ineffective courses of action with something better. The opinion writer needs to suggest an alternative where one exists. This can improve the department's credibility with the area asking for help even if the proposed way forward would not actually work in practice. Compliance needs to learn what does. So, negative or critical responses to their practical suggestions always assist in that respect.

The compliance department should always strive to avoid having the reputation of being the business prevention unit. Having said that, Compliance needs the courage to produce the "no" hammer and advise that there is no acceptable or safe way around the problem. The person asking the question may actually be looking for that type of opinion.

Compliance ought to develop links with both regulators and others in similar organisations. It cannot know everything within its scope. Sometimes, the correct response will be to instruct outside lawyers (typically about the scope of regulation or legal matters) or compliance specialists. Often, a quick phone call to a contact within the industry may produce the answer or necessary insight.

A firm asked a compliance consultant and lawyer for his view of a particular deal. Rather than expressing a view, he asked: What is the purpose of the transaction? Is it to evade the introduction of the retail distribution review?" (This review involved a significant set of rule changes about to come into force at the time.) On receiving a positive answer, the adviser replied: "Don't do it. Give me half an hour and I'll come back to you with the rules you will be breaking." Another firm was subsequently fined for doing the same transaction.

7

TRAINING

Training should always form part of the compliance advice process. This should include examples of how the rules and the internal procedures apply to the actual issues faced by those present. Abstract learning rarely changes behaviour.

Experts on compliance may not be natural teachers. They can always engage outsiders to deliver the sessions. However, they must attend and participate actively in training that affects their areas (regardless of who commissions it). Sometimes, compliance people fail to turn up, sending to everyone else the destructive message that they do not feel part of the process of observing the rulebook or are just not interested in learning or the topic concerned.

Often, one suspects, this absenteeism stems from a fear that training will expose people's ignorance. However, engaging in the learning process with other departments shows that Compliance has nothing to fear from discovering new things about the business and the rules that apply to it.

> Attending courses where Marketing tackles advertising regulation issues helps Compliance to master not just the range of applicable rules but the practicalities of different forms of communication. It may wish to ban the use of a social media which does not generate its own records. It cannot do so without knowing the name of the medium concerned (Snapchat).

Without attending and learning, how can surveillance efforts target the right things – the matters of substance that can easily go wrong and cause major problems – rather than the easy-to-spot but trivial rule breaches?

There is a further important point. Compliance cannot afford to miss an occasion when a trainer from another department or from outside the company presents a message which is inconsistent with its own view. It has to have people in the room able to challenge the opinion being expressed. If the training process exposes the fact that the company has been doing something wrongly because of a weakness in its policies and controls, Compliance needs to know about this as quickly as possible and put things right.

8

MONITORING

8.1 Introduction

Monitoring lies at the heart of every compliance department's activities. What people do not know, they cannot fix. This activity involves gathering information from a variety of sources and through a range of techniques and approaches. A whisper in a staff canteen (followed up by an in-depth investigation!) can prove far more informative than a deep-dive file review.

8.2 Fundamental standards

Compliance's ability to receive insights from around the business drives the success or otherwise of its activities. Its presence and availability to advise and help in other ways gives it access to material that it needs for its monitoring activities. People doing this job have to meet people of all ranks in the organisation, make it clear how easy they are to contact and act discreetly to protect their sources. Participating actively in work-related activities such as training, and mixing with people throughout the organisation, opens access to information. Compliance departments that stick to themselves cannot possibly monitor effectively.

> One organisation had a problem with the delivery of a valuable free gift to new customers. Internal Audit thought that this had been resolved. A training course delivered by an outside consultant revealed that middle management who absented themselves from the session had decided not to record complaints about this problem, giving the false impression that it had disappeared. It was healthy that staff on the ground could share this information and worrying and an indicator of wider issues that absent middle-managers had effectively misled Internal Audit.

Monitoring has to observe certain fundamental standards. The most important and most honoured in the breach is the no-retaliation rule. The second general principle which can wrongly be understood to undermine the first is that usually systems, process and management by senior managers cause or allow errors and misbehaviour, not individuals.

8.2.1 No retaliation

The "no-retaliation" rule applies to every individual in the organisation. Any breach of it should be a ground for immediate dismissal. In the UK and elsewhere, whistleblowing laws expose the organisation to litigation from employees treated less well because they made a protected disclosure. Compliance has a duty to minimise the risk of breaches in this area by communicating this requirement to and enforcing it against everyone of all ranks and by reducing unnecessary disclosures of sources of information. Even if whistleblowing rules did not exist, the department would need a culture of open and regular disclosure of issues by front-line staff in order to function properly.

It is unreasonable to expect everyone within an organisation to like each other. Many of the more critical disclosures can be driven by less than pure motives. (Regulators report that most of their information comes from competitors to the relevant firms.) However, motivation can only be of marginal relevance to Compliance. Given information about something that could be material, this department has to investigate and see for itself whether complaints about a department or individual are justified.

The organisation sometimes needs to know why such levels of hostility exist. Mismanagement or the placing of any inappropriate individual either in charge or just in the team often explains why junior staff tell compliance or audit functions about things going wrong in their team. Good managers rarely "inspire" their teams to complain about them.

Individual staff members do not always have a full picture of what is happening. So, a proper detailed eyes-open look at one issue may flush out other concerns about the business of even greater importance.

The temptation in this area for both companies and regulators is to bring in an external consultant to do the review work which may just entail repeating Compliance's view. Unfortunately, the outside firm has an interest in not being too brutal about the firm and its senior management for fear of losing future business. A report from Compliance to the Board, particularly the non-executive directors, has a far greater chance of being both accurate and relevant to the organisation. Chief Executives find it embarrassing to fire the entire compliance function.

Most entities should aim for a culture where people can tell Compliance of their concerns anonymously. In practice, all too few achieve anything like this. Compliance needs a detailed procedure for the discreet handling of what the UK Employment Rights Act 1996 calls protected disclosures. Section 43B introduced by the Public Interest Disclosure Act 1998 defines these as any information disclosure which the discloser reasonably believes "tends to show one of":

- a crime or miscarriage of justice "has been..., is being... or is likely to be committed;
- anyone "has failed, is failing or is likely to fail to comply with any legal obligation";
- any individual's health or safety or the environment "has been, is being or is likely to be endangered"; or
- the current or likely future deliberate concealment of such a fact.

Organisations need processes for handling such information because otherwise they risk breaking the law by limiting the right to make such disclosures. Some use external third parties to handle whistleblowing for this reason.

It is an ugly fact of life that the most effective whistleblowers are not the people you read about, but those who discreetly allow key people to know what is going on. When they realise that the organisation is doing nothing about the problem, they change jobs "because it is time to move on" and tell the relevant regulator what has happened.

A failure by a manager or compliance person to make this type of regulatory disclosure will expose the individual to enforcement action on the basis that they acquiesced in or failed to tell the regulator what was going on.

8.2.2 Systems and senior managers usually cause problems not other individuals

The second principle – that systems, corporate culture and senior managers cause problems not individuals – can sometimes feel almost as difficult to observe as the "no retaliation" principle. Many of us have looked into the eyes of someone who just does not understand why what they have done is unacceptable. It is vital that the organisation removes that individual from a position of responsibility as quickly as possible. Compliance has to recommend that clearly. However, that does not absolve the person that allowed or perhaps even instructed such staff members to do what they did. The bad apple approach can disguise much more serious problems.

> An advice firm found itself in serious regulatory trouble, apparently due to the activities of one adviser who had recommended a substantial number of his customers to invest in an unregulated investment scheme. A more in-depth investigation revealed that a number of directors of the company had given a number of similar recommendations. The real issue or cause of the problem was a culture of encouraging advisers to do what they felt was best without meaningful controls. The company recovered from its problem by addressing that issue after the miscreant adviser had left.

8.2.3 Further monitoring principles

Proper compliance needs three more monitoring principles. First, nothing and nobody is off limits. The chief executive can just as easily break the rules as anyone else and often has more opportunities to do so in significant ways. Secondly, the monitoring plan does not represent the limits of the team's activities. Intelligence gathered through external and internal sources, both formal and otherwise may prove more important.

Finally, Compliance should never be "marking its own homework" unless there is no alternative. A small organisation, which simply cannot have front-line compliance people and a separate team monitoring them, may have to compromise here or use external or internal audit functions to check on Compliance's work. However, normally, in the absence of proper external scrutiny, everyone will perceive that Compliance is protecting its own reputation. This may sometimes reflect reality. In fact, without the detachment of an outsider's view, it can be difficult to see exactly how Compliance performed when things go wrong.

> In the "bad apple" example just described, an external review started from the position that the compliance monitoring must have failed. After a study of six years of Board minutes, it reached a different conclusion. Compliance (both internal and external) regularly drew the directors' attention to the problem but lacked the resources, authority and encouragement to do anything practical about it. The board and executive's approach to Compliance rather than the other way around was central to what had happened.

So, armed with a culture of openness and a compliance function ready and willing to hear from different parts of the organisation, with strict no-retaliation rules, and an emphasis on seeking out weaknesses in the organisation and senior management, not lowly individuals, the team is ready to monitor what is happening.

8.3 Designing the monitoring plan

There has to be a monitoring plan to ensure that formal monitoring happens. The classic approach is to throw the largest amount of resource into checking things that create the biggest risk for the organisation. However, monitoring must also cover the breadth of the organisation's activities. Otherwise, Compliance risks missing developing issues and creating a permissive culture in areas perceived to be less dangerous.

Depending on the business's size, one can create a number of different categories requiring equivalent levels of scrutiny. In practice, one needs a two-speed approach: for obviously high-risk issues and business as usual. In larger organisations, one will typically need more categories within, and fluidity between, these two types of activity.

8.3.1 High-risk monitoring

The main focus must be where activities pose the highest risk to the business and its compliance: typically the more dangerous areas and where the entity is most active. Compliance has to know the business well enough to identify both segments. A knowledge of what the organisation is doing, where and how and the state of its regulatory authorisations should enable monitoring to identify risk levels and sensible ways of checking behaviour. This has to be Compliance's assessment. The business must not persuade it to oversee lightly activities which generate a large proportion of the organisation's revenue.

The nature of the organisation and the areas in which it operates will drive the identification of major risk factors. Significant incentives, both financial and personal, to achieve certain transaction volumes always increase the temptations or drives towards particular outcomes. This is particularly true where the compliant result clashes with the organisation's sales goals. Where the business has significantly increased its sales of a particular product type or wants to do so, Compliance has to ask whether the organisation missed the needs of large numbers of customers for this the first time or whether it is just selling things to people who do not need them.

In 2019, the Financial Conduct Authority fined Prudential Assurance and Standard Life a total of almost £55 million and expected it to pay a further £311 million in compensation to customers. Each company significantly incentivised staff to ring customers as they reached retirement age to persuade them to buy their pension income (typically an annuity) from their companies while not giving advice. It should not have surprised either company that its sales force failed to give the full disclosure required by the regulator of the customers' right to shop elsewhere and the likelihood that they would receive more money that way.

Selling complex products by telephone without giving advice is almost impossible to do. Both companies should have been monitoring their telephone lines daily. The sales incentives for persuading many customers to act against their own best interests needed to have been blocked. This highly toxic situation required either intense monitoring or, better, advice from Compliance to stop the whole activity.

Compliance needs to know the regulator's concerns and increase the intensity of monitoring to match it. For example, within nine months of starting its regulation of payment protection insurance in 2005, the Financial Services Authority expressed concerns about the way in which firms were selling this product. Firms that stopped sales straightaway saved themselves millions or billions of pounds. Previously, the Financial Ombudsman Service had expressed concerns about irresponsible lending to people unable to maintain the necessary payments.

> Cattles plc, a company that no longer exists, said in its 2006 Annual Report that sales of payment protection insurance (PPI) represented about 11% of revenues and noted below market trend levels of arrears on its consumer lending business. Its business basically consisted of three high-risk subjects: PPI and loan sales to consumers who might have difficulties with their repayments and dealing with arrears issues.

Compliance needs a strategy for looking at each higher risk area: to detect what may have gone wrong or could well do so in the future. A mystery shopping plan can flush out some of the worst areas. Telephone sales, particularly where staff have incentives to close transactions but cannot give advice, call for in-depth critical listening to significant volumes of recordings by Compliance, not just the leaders of the sales teams. Monitors need to check for any traces of a recommendation, a clear statement that no advice is being given, and any comments that could be regarded as not being "clear, fair and not misleading".

Regulators have fined firms for a whole range of sales techniques, notably assuming that the customer wants to buy an add-on product or challenging the customer's rejection or cancellation of the insurance. Both constitute advice. Another danger area involves the situation where the customer has rejected the idea of entering into the contract, and yet somehow has ended up having money taken from their account for this.

Material levels of non-compliance in all these areas will need to be escalated quickly and raise questions about the business model being used.

A common high-risk area with financial advice concerns organisations whose customers almost routinely seem to end up taking the same unorthodox high-risk action as a result of the firm's recommendations. Doing transfers from employers' pension schemes or investing in unregulated collective investment schemes provide two well-known examples. We need regular individual detailed file checks when that type of thing happens.

Recommendations of potentially risky products should regularly attract detailed monitoring even though they can be perfectly justified if the customers' circumstances fit.

> With a typical lifetime mortgage, elderly customers do not make payments on their mortgage, but the lender adds the interest to the capital borrowed and everything has to be repaid on the property's sale, typically on death or a move to a care home. When people with no family borrow a small amount each year, this can work well. However, there is a real risk of advisers recommending customers to borrow far more than they need. By doing this, the firms concerned can earn more remuneration from recommending investments for the sums unnecessarily "released". Family members can be horrified to learn that their parents' apparent largest asset, their home, is worthless on their death. Extra checks can save firms major problems with them and the regulator.

Where advice has been offered or given, one expects to find proper reports documenting the recommendation, the link or links between it and the facts which the client has presented, and an explanation of the risks involved. This type of box-ticking, though, is not enough. Good monitoring focuses more on whether the recommendation looks right and whether outcomes reached make sense in relation to the customers involved. To do this form of work, qualification as a financial adviser or something equivalent, such as an accountant or actuary, should be compulsory.

More mainstream financial advice can be covered in business as usual monitoring with a focus on advisers with more complex clients, a reputation for sloppy work or the way that the individual's large business volumes pose a higher risk to the business.

8.3.2 Business as usual monitoring

Compliance also needs a business-as-usual plan which again classifies the organisation's activities by risk level, devoting resources correspondingly, but now aims for a broader look at the whole organisation. It needs this to improve standards generally, update its own risk categorisation and spot new issues as they emerge. Significant problems found in particular areas will increase their risk level within this type of monitoring and may elevate the activity to the higher risk categories.

As before, Compliance's description of the organisation's activities, products and services helps it to create and update priorities and decide how it will examine each activity.

8.3.2.1 Governance

Monitoring should begin with the organisation's governance. As indicated earlier, Compliance checks, as part of its annual regulatory returns, that the organisation and its key individuals have the necessary registrations or authorisations to carry out its activities in the various parts of the world where they occur and the legally required capital to do so. Reading the minutes provides some reassurance that the Board is functioning properly and considering compliance issues.

Beyond that lies a string of uncomfortable questions about the apportionment of responsibility. Do all the senior managers perform the roles formally expected of them? Do accountability chains make sense? Does everyone have a proper job description? Can they identify what they are supposed to be doing and the individuals to whom they are answerable?

As we saw earlier, some organisations do not realise or turn a blind eye to the fact that they have shadow directors or executives, people who really run the organisation without having the necessary titles. Occasionally, the "shadow" may have a criminal record or other (typically solvency) problems which would preclude their being a director. In less-well-publicised instances, external advisers become so powerful because of their client's dependence on them that they are in effect running the organisation. Routine involvement in and presence at decision-making meetings may persuade Compliance to warn of a shadow director risk. Where people holding certain positions need regulatory approval before taking their position, an unapproved individual doing the job creates significant regulatory issues for both that person and the organisation. It also makes it difficult to see clearly lines of accountability within the business.

8.3.2.2 Products, services and their marketing

Compliance then looks at the products and services to see whether they have been properly designed to produce outcomes consistent with regulatory requirements. In a consumer-focused activity, this extends beyond eligibility questions to the needs of an accurately identified group of targeted customers. Elsewhere, what is done has to meet certain standards towards both clients and the market.

Compliance can often sample one obvious area, marketing, by just acting as consumers, following the organisation's various social media accounts, checking its website and looking at more traditional promotions.

Often, success (from a compliance perspective) stems from remaining "outside" the rulebooks. Brand names and logos presented in public places without comment usually meet this requirement. However, anything that mentions the quality of the product or service or invites the customer to purchase risks breaching "clear, fair and not misleading" requirements. In some areas such as consumer credit, these are eye-wateringly tight. Compliance needs to understand how they apply to the printed page. If the firm needs rule waivers from the relevant authorities, the same team will probably end up leading the application process by explaining to the regulator how the rules' strict application prevents sensible legitimate marketing. Particularly strict regulation can require firms to reclassify upwards the risk and carry out more detailed checking of certain promotional activity.

By monitoring marketing activity on social media and elsewhere, Compliance can discover things about the organisation which it needs to stop or alter.

> Standard Life was fined and paid over £100 million in compensation for a promotion for its pension sterling fund in 2010. A graph on the offending factsheet showed about five downward movements in the fund's performance between 2007 and 2008. If Compliance had noticed this, it could have warned management that the fund was not invested 100% in cash or cash-like instruments as the promotion suggested, but was in something that responded erratically to concerns about the mortgage-backed securities market. (It held significant investments in those type of assets.)
>
> A bank's checking of Twitter accounts picked up a sponsorship of a beer festival. This raised a whole range of cultural and antisocial behaviour issues. The person who spotted the "tweet" was also and perhaps primarily concerned with the fact that the bank's sponsorship committee had never approved the association.

Monitoring now has to examine service or product delivery. Often, this involves examining outsourcing arrangements including whether activities central to the organisation should be outsourced at all.

8.3.2.2.1 Outsourcing

Compliance should have been consulted on any service-level standards and agreements. It needs to check that they remain appropriate and that the organisation adequately checks the outsourcer's work. The team also needs to ensure that we could take over the outsourced activities if the outside body encountered difficulties. At the same time, monitoring should ask whether a regulator can gain sufficient access to the outsourcer to enable it to supervise the relevant operations. A large organisation might usefully have a team dedicated to monitoring outsourcing arrangements. Compliance could then check its effectiveness.

8.3.2.2.2 Checking delivery of the organisation's offering

Compliance monitoring has to focus on the delivery of the organisations' primary functions. For insurers, this means claims decisions. Compliance needs to check partial and full rejection decisions and the reasons given for them. Due amounts must be paid promptly to the right people.

> A purpose of taking out life insurance should be to enable loved ones to pay for funeral expenses and other immediate costs that arise when people die, without having to wait for probate to be granted. Some companies have a policy of refusing to pay out until probate has been granted which rather defeats the point of the exercise and almost certainly breaches the contract. They also do not consider why policies were not put in trust or set up otherwise to enable immediate payments to be made to the deceased's intended beneficiaries. Compliance needs to review these procedures and override existing processes where life assurance beneficiaries become annoyed at them. They then have to work out why life cover has not been properly put in trust for the intended beneficiaries, so that the sum assured can be paid on proof of the relevant death.

Other contract performance "pinch points" depend on the nature of the organisation. A charity's compliance function needs to review decisions made to allocate funds to higher risk causes and the reasoning behind them, and check that the people making the decisions do not have inappropriate links to the recipients.

> A credit union was shut down after it lent substantial sums to a powerful member. His inability to repay made the union insolvent. Lending decisions to key participants, particularly where they involve substantial amounts, need to be subject to particular compliance scrutiny for obvious conflicts of interest reasons.

Lenders' compliance teams should always monitor carefully their firms' handling of customers in arrears. Both legal and compliance rules insist on businesses going through a number of stages, typically involving some form of forbearance, before any enforcement action. Compliance monitoring should also check the original lending decisions in these cases to see if the customers could reasonably have been expected to repay the debt: a growing compliance issue.

8.3.2.3 Looking at compliance people's work

Monitoring can force Compliance to review its own team members' work. Typically, the product governance committee or its equivalent will have a compliance person on it to insist on changes to any product or service proposal and ensure that the body abides by the procedures. Second line monitoring of the type described here cannot tread softly just because it is scrutinising the work of someone in its team. For a whole range of reasons, including ignorance and being blindsided by other parts of the product development process, Compliance makes mistakes.

8.3.2.4 Checking senior managers' work

The same issues apply to the monitoring of senior managers' work. This has to be sampled and checked at least as vigorously as less influential individuals. Bosses typically pose far greater risks to the organisation, through their influence and often the higher sensitivity or just volume of work that they do. Obstruction of that process should generate concerns about the appropriateness of certain individuals to hold senior positions.

8.3.3 Complaints

Compliance monitoring should always cover certain standard areas where detailed rules create the likelihood of rule breaches, or one learns about issues elsewhere in the organisation. For both reasons, checks should always cover complaint handling. UK and EU rules and international standards cover this subject in detail. In addition, good teams in this area will flush out many of the customer care issues of which Compliance needs to be aware.

By the same token, any malfunctioning part of the process can prevent the organisation from being able to resolve issues encountered by customers and learn from its mistakes. Equally, though, there are inherent conflicts of interest involved here. Upholding complaints typically involves the organisation paying compensation.

Complaints monitoring should cover each of the stages of the complaints process:

- Is it easy to identify how to complain – typically through a website which gives also the name of any external Ombudsman or other dispute resolution arrangements?
- Does the organisation apply consistently a clear appropriate definition of a complaint?
- Are complaints correctly identified and recorded (without considering their merits)?
- Do complainants receive appropriate acknowledgement if immediate resolution cannot be achieved?
- Are investigators of cases that are not purely about simple clerical matters as neutral as practicable and ideally not from the team complained about?
- Do investigations cover both what the customer referred to and what someone with inside knowledge would have known that they ought to have complained about?
- Do investigators show inappropriate tendencies to believe people from within the organisation in preference to complainants, at least, without good reason?

- Are decisions fair and reasonable, considering what the organisation knows about its practices and weaknesses – judged by both in-house criteria and those of any dispute resolution body such as an Ombudsman?
- Has anyone imposed any constraints on decision-makers apart from reasonably generous limits beyond which payments require approval?
- Can customers, dispute resolution bodies and regulators understand the response to the complaint, the basis for the decision and what the former can and should do next?
- What lessons have been learnt from complaints?
- Are complaint records and reports to regulators and other bodies within a reasonable distance of being accurate?

> In 2015, Lloyds Banking Group paid a £117 million fine for telling its complaint handling staff to assume that its sales of payment protection insurance followed the rules when its own root cause analysis and compliance suggested otherwise.

The key is to focus here on what matters. If the organisation does not identify complaints correctly, it loses any record of them, fails to resolve complainants' issues and produces wildly misleading data for the business (the ultimate garbage-in-garbage-out example) generally and for regulatory reporting purposes. For this reason, an increase in complaints can be a good sign. Similarly, low levels of complaints and rule-breach identification can demonstrate a weak compliance culture generally. A healthy business facilitates complaints and their resolution. Auditing this requires a combination of mystery shopping and checking all standard means of complaining, notably by listening to call centre telephone recordings and reading email and social media traffic.

Most enforcement action relates to the fairness of decisions and the quality of investigations. As the Lloyds example and others show, this involves sampling complaint rejections to check the merits of the response and whether the investigator had taken reasonable steps to establish what happened and why. It is less important to check whether the firm misreported to the regulator the time taken to resolve a case: a "low-hanging fruit" area for Compliance but not one where a UK financial services regulator has ever taken enforcement action.

8.3.4 Financial crime and money laundering

A permanent monitoring item should cover financial crime and money laundering prevention. Sanctions emerging from the Russian invasion of Ukraine and the EU Fourth and Fifth Money Laundering Directives have moved this subject beyond financial services businesses to art dealers and antique booksellers.

Any organisation should identify its financial crime risks and have procedures to guard against them. Monitoring must check those documents and staff awareness of and ability to implement them. This could include considering the paper trail where the organisation declined to do business with someone, reported them to the authorities, increased internal monitoring of accounts or just escalated concerns to the money laundering reporting officer. Compliance also needs to check staff training records and take the courses concerned themselves, not just to ensure that they have attended but to verify that the programmes reach the required content and accessibility standards.

In the last decade, substantial numbers of financial institutions of all sizes have had "remediation" projects designed to redo the due diligence and ongoing monitoring done in relation to their clients. Compliance should probably start to plan their monitoring activities by consulting some of those involved in these projects. Routine compliance sampling should have picked up much of the rework involved through checking documentation surrounding "know your customer work" and the management of cases which ought to have been escalated to the money laundering reporting officer by front-line staff.

8.3.5 Human resources (HR)

Workplace environment monitoring can be more controversial. An independent audit function may do this better. Someone, though, needs to tell management when an organisation located in an ethnically diverse area seems to have a work force that does not reflect this. Compliance can identify other diversity recruitment issues and deliver to senior management any race or gender pay gap data if HR has not already done this. This is necessary for the organisation to avoid both corporate groupthink and employment law litigation. Compliance should anyway have clear agreements with the audit function on who will be monitoring human resources issues within the organisation and how the two departments will share information.

8.4 Monitoring techniques

Most monitoring techniques are fairly obvious and some have been mentioned already, like listening to tapes and sampling advice files. Otherwise, management information (MI), the mapping of activities of the business area by the team concerned against the relevant rules and procedure items, file checks, interviewing people and just being around and listening and watching all provide insight. We need, though, some scepticism about any source.

Materials selected by managers for review will often be cherry-picked to make the team look better than it is. Random selection by the monitoring team works much better. Compliance has to select or at least challenge the MI, not the department or senior management. For example, low levels of complaints or compensation paid in response to concerns about insurance claims decisions may reflect customers' difficulty in contacting the company with its dissatisfaction or automatic decisions to uphold the claims department's decisions. Random checks on actual cases would work much better.

8.5 Using monitoring information

Compliance needs to report any significant information gathered through monitoring to management in a detailed reasoned form, using clear criteria for any opinions expressed consistently across the organisation. The report may itself explain further investigations triggered by the team's findings. Above all else, though, it should contain clear recommendations. However, there is no reason not to discuss with relevant staff and managers any findings and what is being suggested before the report goes in. It is particularly important for Compliance to discuss negative monitoring observations and recommendations for change with the team concerned. There may be very good reasons for what has happened. Compliance could have misunderstood something or the monitored department might have been following instructions from elsewhere or been deprived of the resources required. Sometimes, these types of discussions reveal failings elsewhere in the organisation that now need investigation.

The same type of discussion should surround any proposed changes. Compliance needs to avoid setting unreasonable goals that either conflict with instructions from elsewhere in the organisation or misuse resources.

Ultimately, though, Compliance must have the final word in its monitoring reports. They need to explain the team's conclusions in much the same way as the written opinions discussed earlier. They also have to set out what Compliance has done, both formally and otherwise and what it has discovered. Any suggested changes to behaviours or procedures or other concerns should be supported by detailed reasoning with reference to external sources, typically published regulatory views.

Compliance and Internal Audit often grade the outcomes of their investigations. It might be more useful to prioritise necessary changes or improvements rather than a red, amber or green rating of a team's work based on what may be quite limited material. It can be unnecessarily discouraging and unhelpful for a team to hear of its previous work's unsatisfactory grade when it knows that the company's managers, through their policies or allocation of resources, have prevented it from doing its job properly.

Reports should be presented to the relevant level of the organisation, typically the Board, notably if Compliance fears that its recommendations will not be followed. Compliance needs to put down a marker of the standards that it considers the organisation should meet to protect itself against regulatory action. This also ensures that responsibility for rejecting its conclusions stands firmly with the person or people making that decision.

A major issue in all this work concerns the competence and credibility of monitors. Only people with the relevant qualifications and technical knowledge should be seen to be making major decisions or recommendations. Otherwise, the department can dismiss Compliance as incompetent meddlers and will probably receive management support in doing so and rejecting any changes. Sometimes, for that reason, the monitoring team may sometimes need an external second opinion.

Follow-up monitoring of agreed alterations to behaviour is vital to ensure that the monitoring process achieves its goals. It can also be necessary to ensure that the agreed changes have not created a different set of issues for the organisation.

9

SIGNING THINGS OFF – FIRST LINE COMPLIANCE

Compliance uses far less resource if the organisation does things correctly the first time. However, excessive scrutiny of everything the firm does would stop anything productive from happening. Instead, one generally relies on a combination of advice, monitoring and procedures to maintain acceptable standards. Sometimes, though, an activity has sufficient importance that a business needs to check things before they go out.

Financial services regulators across Europe and beyond require or expect this type of "sign-off" before firms launch new products or significant adaptations of them and any significant promotional activity.

The compliance or risk functions have to be involved in the arrangements for launching and reviewing providers' offerings to the public. In some organisations, Compliance attends all the meetings but does not have a vote or veto power and so preserves its ability to review the product governance arrangements. This does not really work. The company needs to know if it is about to break the rules or is likely to do so in the future and understand how it can shape what it offers or how it distributes this in order to remain on the "right side" of the line. The compliance person on this type of committee should vote and have an unofficial veto power. Another option which can and probably should be combined with the previous one, is for the product development team to engage the main compliance department for advice on its designs. The proposition can only be submitted when that department has cleared it. Compliance's involvement, though, in making decisions about products in this way compromises the same department's monitoring of the whole process.

The best that one can do is to have different people involved in being the first and second line compliance people in this area. In smaller firms, where there may not be enough people for this purpose, the audit function performs the second line function.

Financial promotions pose a slightly different range of problems. First, one has to distinguish between the almost identical ideas of approving a promotion and signing it off. In the UK, it is essentially a crime to issue an invitation or inducement to do anything regulated by the FCA in the course of business. There are three key exceptions to this: the person communicating is authorised by that regulator, the promotion has been approved by someone who is authorised or the Financial Promotions Order exempts the communication from this prohibition.

In this context, approval by an authorised firm constitutes a step required for an unregulated business to communicate the material. Recent concerns about higher-risk investment promotions approved by regulated businesses have led the Financial Conduct Authority (FCA) to expand its requirements for these types of approvals and the UK Government to create an authorisation process for approvers.

Even when the issuer of the promotion is FCA-authorised, regulators not unreasonably expect companies to do some form of checking or "sign-off" before they publish major promotions, although they have not officially required this for some time (in part to enable the use of social media). Traditionally, financial institutions often gave the sign-off job to Compliance.

Increasingly, though, firms now build the sign-off process into the marketing department to enable Compliance to monitor this process independently. In practice, though, someone is signing things off or rejecting or insisting on the rewriting of material by reference to the regulators' rules. To describe them as not doing a compliance job seems almost perverse! The compliance department then oversees that person's decisions as part of its promotions monitoring. This seems to work.

10

BOARD REPORTING

Like most components of modern organisations, Compliance has to manage up as well as down. In a financial services business where the department's work is central to the organisation's long-term success, its report should be a standing item at every Board meeting. In any event, Compliance needs to tell both the Board and meetings of senior executives anything significant that it has learned through its ongoing monitoring or study of external developments, such as proposed rule or legislative changes.

Since 2007, the EU directives and regulations on investment business have required, for firms within their scope, regular and at least annual reports to the Board on compliance, business risk and anything identified through internal audits. From the start, these needed to cover "the implementation and effectiveness of the overall control environment, risks identified and any complaint handling issues".[1] Now, on top of this, at least annually, firms must supply information about products made and sold by the firm, the distribution strategy and any other services they supply. Guidelines issued by the European Securities and Markets Authority (ESMA) supply a useful list of topics to be covered in these and similar documents. This starts by describing the compliance team and its activities:

- a summary of the team's structure, personnel numbers, qualifications, reporting lines and any changes to this during the reporting period; and

- monitoring methods and how the team goes about identifying possible compliance risks, including future monitoring plans.

The report then looks outwards at material regulatory developments, a summary of any communications with regulators and new significant compliance issues.

Compliance then needs to describe the result of monitoring and reviews, covering:

- any major findings and "risks identified",
- problems with the firm's "organisation and compliance process";
- a view of the "effectiveness of the ... policies and procedures"; and
- steps taken to handle any significant risk of compliance failure.

The report takes a detour into complaints received, things learnt from them and action taken as a result. It then concludes, perhaps over-idealistically, by suggesting disclosure of:

- any failure by senior management to follow "important recommendations or assessments by compliance"; and
- any instances where other business units have tried to instruct or inappropriately influence Compliance.

According to ESMA, separate reports to the Board on product governance need to cover:

- Compliance's role in drafting and reviewing policies and procedures
- major breaches and actions to be taken to fix them

- the "number and nature of the products manufactured or distributed",
- their target markets
- other material from the product approval process needed to consider the compliance risks involved – complexity, conflicts of interests, product testing data and cost-return ratios, including a particular look at new or significant amended products; and
- the distribution strategy and distributors used, again with a particular focus on new ones; and
- the extent to which products have been sold outside their target market.

Since 31 July 2023, the UK Financial Conduct Authority has required another compliance report to be made to the Board for firms dealing with retail customers which can encompass the product material just described. It now, though, has to extend to communications with and customer support supplied to "retail customers". The report covers the firm's monitoring of the "Consumer Duty" imposed on financial services businesses with these types of clients. It deals with the questions of whether:

- products sold in the past or currently are designed to meet the "needs, characteristics and objectives" of those who have them,
- products "provide fair value" and, if not, what has been done about this,
- customers have the "right information to make effective, timely and properly informed decisions ... and ... receive the support they need",

- one group of retail clients has had a different experience with the same product from another and the business has harmed "any retail customers".

Finally, the report must cover the root causes of any problems discovered.

Uncomfortably, once the Board has received the report, it then has to issue its own, probably in practice drafted by Compliance. This requires confirmation of whether the firm is complying with the Consumer Duty rules and considers whether its future strategy matches this. The Board report has to agree any actions designed to ensure that the firm does not break the Duty and address past problems and any necessary business strategy changes.

Where this is a significant issue, the money laundering reporting officer should at least annually report to the Board and Executive Committee on the effectiveness of controls in that area.

One of the trickiest areas concerns a further compliance report to the Board on whistleblowing which has to cover the effectiveness of the firm's systems while protecting individual whistleblowers' anonymity.

Any business could use the examples of these reports as at least a starting point. Most financial services firms should follow the blueprint provided. There is a danger, though, that this process may become a tick-box exercise for both Compliance and senior management. The former still needs to read the Board minutes with care to ensure that its report is attached or its contents appear in the account of the discussions.

---

1. The now superseded articles 22 and 25 of the MiFID Delegated Regulation.

11

ROOT CAUSE ANALYSIS

11.1 Two types

Root cause analysis typically has to be done in two connected areas. First, where monitoring reveals regulatory or legal breaches or unsatisfactory outcomes generally, it makes sense to find out what lies behind the problem. In that way, the organisation can address the key issues that brought about the issue that has surfaced. Secondly, regulators insist that firms examine the root causes of customer complaints. In both cases, where a major issue appears to be broader than just human error, regulators expect changes to be made, and sometimes, if necessary, compensation to be paid to people who have lost out as a result of the incident who may never have complained.

11.2 Differences between complaints and Compliance root cause analysis

There are significant differences between monitoring and complaints root cause analysis. The first type almost certainly sits within the compliance department's responsibility. It discovered the problem and, as part of its monitoring, has to dig deeper to find out what lies behind it. Nobody else typically picks up this type of work.

With complaints, the people who handled the case often have the clearest view of what went wrong. Customer relations or whichever team deals with customer dissatisfaction probably should take the lead in this area. Having said that, at least one EU Regulation[1] requires Compliance to "analyse complaints and complaints-handling data to ensure that they identify and address any risks or issues." This all may end up as a joint effort.

Real root cause analysis could put the spotlight firmly on Compliance's decision to allow or even encourage the behaviour that has generated the problem. While that department has to monitor all aspects of complaints work, it can find itself "marking its own homework" and consequently obstructing the effective analysis of complaints. For that reason, Internal audit can be the better team to take charge here.

Complaints work here may look beyond compliance issues, particularly where the firm correctly rejected the complaint. Analysis can, for example, focus on why the firm did business with the client concerned when their personality or circumstances did not fit the organisation.

11.3 A more unified concept of root cause analysis

The Financial Conduct Authority summarises the root cause analysis task (in complaint handling) as identifying and remedying recurring or systemic problems. We can use this in all such analysis. Whoever does this work needs to split "identifying" and "remedying" in order to prevent the enormity of a potential solution from affecting the identification of widespread problems. Remedial action will probably require decisions to be made at Exco or Board level.

The regulator gives us a list of four identification tasks:[2]

- identifying complaints' or compliance problems' root causes;
- analysing "the causes of individual complaints" or compliance breaches to "identify root causes common to types of" such cases;

- considering whether these "causes could also affect other processes or products"; and
- collecting management information on causes of complaints and compliance problems and the products and services concerned.

At this point, we need to ask some awkward questions about "root causes". The concept of a "cause" is basically a philosophical one. Most events have multiple "causes". We are actually looking for meaningful pieces of information about things that have happened from which we can learn. Whether an occurrence "caused" or had no effect on a disaster makes no difference in this context. An organisation needs to identify its major weaknesses in order to address them, take them into account in its decision-making and reduce the likelihood of repetition.

The literature discusses some of the techniques for doing root cause analysis. None is totally satisfactory. "Five-whys" raises the obvious point that identifying why something happened, and why that happened only five times sometimes barely scratches the surface and puts an artificial limit on the enquiry. Protocols used following various medical incidents present a number of features: the need for both a structure and the involvement of everyone who may be able to cast some light on what happened and why. A key is not to regard the event that triggered the problem as the main cause. Physical, organisational and human elements may have combined over a long period to position the entity to have its disastrous moment. Many of the more attractive ideas here share the idea of a search for "actions" and "conditions" and an invitation to all participants to suggest an explanation and any evidence to support their views.

In a large organisation, handling thousands of complaints and similar numbers of compliance issues, assembling everyone involved to examine a series of unconnected incidents will not work. The analyst is really searching for issues that are coming up with particular types of products or services, not just the predominant problem that triggered the complaint or compliance concern.

In this sense, we are abandoning the search for a cause for something more meaningful. Having discovered an issue, we are now looking for everything we can learn from the experience, regardless of its impact. In a complaint case, the choice of client may not have been good, the client agreement could need improvement, elements of the customer experience may have been unsatisfactory or non-compliant and the company might have misidentified or mishandled the customer's expression of dissatisfaction and handled the case poorly.

The problem with this approach is that it may generate a list of issues too long and difficult for the business to handle. It may be better suited to a look at big one-off events or a deliberate look at things going wrong within a sales and complaints process generally than routine complaint handling. In any event, some prioritisation of the work to be done to address what has been discovered is needed for the analysis to generate useful outcomes.

Regulators will expect the team to look for whatever did most harm to the customer, and try to understand the elements behind it that may be both common to other client situations, products and services. The most damaging behaviour, though, could well have been a decision made by the previous or current management that it is too late for the organisation to reverse.

When a product goes wrong, either because it produces bad outcomes for its target market, large complaint volumes or regulatory interest, Compliance should do a "barrier analysis", in which they check the operation of the product governance process and, in particular, any moments which could have stopped the launch. Any evasion of the required process should trigger an investigation as to how this happened. Compliance needs to look into any pressure imposed to launch a product or service within inappropriate timescales, ignorance of procedures and the inability of product monitoring and compliance teams – through effective contacts within the business – to discover and stop this happening.

Sometimes, finding recurring or systemic issues appears straightforward. When a bank's cashpoint machines fail to dispense money or it fails to collect the correct mortgage payments from thousands of customers, the systemic nature of the problem identifies itself or generates enough complaints to achieve that. Digging further behind the IT issues that typically "cause" these issues should help the organisation prevent a repetition.

> After a well-known scandal, it was widely reported that the bank had failed to install a key piece of software that might have prevented it. The root cause analysis and actions that followed might have looked different if someone had discovered that the IT department had installed the relevant kit but company managers had chosen not to switch it on.

In large organisations, a steady diet of a particular type of complaint (bank charges) can either ring alarm bells or it can perhaps be wrongly dismissed as an incidence of trying to run an enormous business.

Systems, procedures, organisational culture, senior management and (over)powerful individuals tend to create these types of issues. Understanding and changing them if necessary lies at the heart of the task.

At least three things follow from the identification of a problem as recurring or systemic. First, front-line complaint handlers have to be told this so that they do not make assumptions that everything is well in that area. (We saw this with the Lloyds' fine for telling case handlers to assume that its payment protection insurance sales process complied despite its contrary root cause analysis.) Secondly, the organisation needs to decide how to prevent the problem from affecting future business or activities. Thirdly, where customers may have lost out due to the weakness identified, senior management must decide whether and how to compensate customers or change their products to solve the underlying issue. We will deal with this third task later when considering crisis management.

A further task, found in the UK FCA complaint rules, concerns the need to train case handlers about the ultimate outcomes of problems that they have handled and developments in regulatory and Ombudsman practice. Compliance should be communicating many of the same messages to the rest of the business.

---

1. Article 26(7) of the EU MiFID Delegated Regulation
2. DISP 1.3.3R(1)-(2)

12

COMMUNICATING WITH REGULATORS

Regulators typically expect Compliance to provide a link between themselves and the organisation. This takes four main forms. Compliance only really needs to do or take charge of the last type of reporting, although it has to monitor at least the first type.

First, organisations have to file regular submissions containing data, such as complaints and business volumes. Accurate reporting of securities transactions plays a key role in keeping markets clean.

Secondly, regulators try to bridge the gap between themselves and the industries that they supervise by making one-off requests for data and occasionally insight. This can create serious resource problems for small firms. In practice, the authorities usually assume that Compliance will deal with this and firms, partly as a result, tend to select that function to handle these types of questionnaires and requests.

Thirdly, Compliance or other parts of the business may wish to maintain an ongoing dialogue with the authorities, telling them of any changes, identified risks or just thoughts about trends in the business.

Finally, and most dangerously, the requirement to be open and cooperative with the authorities also imposes on the business an obligation to tell the authorities embarrassing details about itself before the regulator discovers them. This can feel like a game of Russian roulette. The problem might never have come to light if Compliance had kept quiet.

Organisations need a sensible approach to communicating with their regulators. The Financial Conduct Authority requires all staff actively involved in the business to be "open and cooperative with" relevant authorities.[1] Its guidance on this rule[2] limits this obligation to a need to answer questions put to them by the regulator in an open way and not obstruct the company's reporting of issues to the regulator.

Only senior managers responsible either for areas where problems emerge or for communicating to the authorities (typically but not exclusively compliance staff) need to proactively report matters. This can be seen from the duty imposed on senior managers to "disclose appropriately any information of which the [regulator would] reasonably expect notice".[3] In practice, firms need to put a senior compliance person in charge of the third type of disclosure in order to create a single channel of communication. None of this should deter staff from whistleblowing directly to the regulator. It just improves coordination.

The key question remains as to what matters the firm needs to report pro-actively. This is easy where a major systemic problem has emerged through dramatically increased complaints volumes covering a single issue or from just being aware of what is happening. Here, active communication can help the firm as much as anyone.

As a result of a systems failure, Clydesdale Bank under-collected significant amounts of mortgage payments over four years. It then tried to recover the lost money by increasing future charges. The Financial Conduct Authority fined it £8.9 million and ordered it to carry out a redress programme that cost much more because the bank had not followed the approach publicly laid down by the Financial Ombudsman Service when it tried to recoup past underpayments. When the bank discovered the problem, it should have contacted the regulator immediately and agreed an approach to the uncollected amounts.

Often, regulators ignore quite significant disclosures, particularly when they do not think that customers have lost out as a result of the compliance breach concerned.

Compliance has to judge carefully when to treat something as a material breach that should be logged in its own systems and reported immediately to the authorities. Everyone makes mistakes. Regulators only want to know material of which it would reasonably expect notice. A significant rule breach differs from harmless inaccuracies. Compliance justifiably makes itself unpopular both internally and at the regulator when it reports failures to write the appropriate letter within eight weeks of receiving a complaint while ignoring the underlying problem that generated the customer dissatisfaction.

The list found in the Financial Conduct Authority's SUP 15.3.11R can help firms decide what they need to tell the regulator. It goes well beyond "significant" conventional rule breaches. Things which may do serious damage to the firm's solvency, legality or reputation that have either happened or are about to occur have to form the subject of detailed disclosures and often direct personal contact with the regulator. The same applies to frauds against customers or the firm, accounting irregularities or other things which show a potential weakness in the business' core systems and controls and an increase in the organisation's risk profile.

---

1. COCON 2.1.3R
2. COCON 4.2.25-29G
3. COCON 2.2.4R

13

HANDLING CRISES

When something goes badly wrong, Compliance will almost certainly play a major role in managing the crisis. Its task may be just to advise senior management or it could involve taking control of the situation. Either way, everyone, including the authorities, expects Compliance to steer the organisation through whatever follows.

Crises blow up one day or simmer gently over a long period of time. As they develop, slow-burning problems should always be disclosed to regulators in as much detail as possible. Usually they have better things on which to focus unless the firm's problems could have a systemic effect on the financial system (typically if it is a bank or significant insurer). This may buy the organisation time to tackle the issues that threaten its survival. Public bodies do not, however, like surprises or feeling that they have been left in the dark. Much of what follows applies to both types of disaster. The difference is that everyone has more time to prepare for the slow-burner occasions.

Compliance has an important role to play in creating the "playbook" for handling the crisis. It may want to begin by imposing some controls on internal communications, such as keeping email or equivalent messages to the absolute minimum, to manage the build-up of panic, misinformation, leaks and other destructive phenomena. Otherwise, the key elements look something like this:

First, the firm has to tell the regulator what has happened as soon as it has worked this out at least in broad terms. A phone call, not just a formal written notification should generate the required attention from the Authority. Setting up a channel of communication with the right person as the events unfurl could prove vital.

Secondly, the organisation must urgently tell its professional indemnity insurers, again in writing and through a call to its brokers. Underwriters like voiding policies for late notifications.

Thirdly, the firm now needs to find out what has really happened by interviewing everyone who might know. This could be described as an accelerated or preliminary form of root cause analysis. This enables the organisation to prepare its reaction to what has occurred, including, where necessary, instructing outside lawyers and compliance help.

While desperately trying to keep the organisation together and handling what may be their own feelings of guilt about failing to stop the issue arising, Compliance and leadership have to listen. Regulators may tell the business what it needs, how and when. Staff caught up in the maelstrom could have key insights as to the weaknesses of the organisation that may have allowed the disaster to occur. Key staff will leave on bad terms if they do not feel that management is tuning into what they have to say.

The fourth stage involves working out the firm's liability or financial exposure for what has happened and its effect on the organisation's solvency. This will usually involve external legal and possibly other advice. Initial disclosures to the regulator create more time for this stage. Once the firm has an idea of the damage for which it is responsible, it can talk sensibly again to the Authority about agreeing any necessary compensation package and the process involved. The firm may have no liabilities flowing from the issue that has arisen. However, the organisation has to think about how, if at all, it is going to change as a result of what has happened (perhaps by losing staff members and business volumes due to the disruption caused). Compliance's management of the regulator will probably depend on this.

Finally, the firm has to show the authorities its acceptance of responsibility for what has happened. Regulators always assume that weaknesses in the organisation's systems and controls lie at the heart of most disasters. An offer to the authorities of an outside review of these and the retraining of key staff can be a game-changer. The Financial Conduct Authority regards this type of suggestion as a form of "mitigation". Authorities find it expensive and uncomfortable to shut businesses. So, showing willingness to improve and subject oneself to outside, if somewhat private, scrutiny often meets their needs better than any enforcement action.

Organisations do not survive all crises and many change their form and type of operation significantly afterwards, sometimes for the better. Compliance (typically a different team to the one that oversaw the creation of the problem in the first place) may have to negotiate a way of managing the business' liabilities with compensation schemes and authorities, typically with significant legal, accounting and insolvency practitioner support. Whatever the outcome, Compliance's management of these incidents can help to protect businesses and the individuals working in them, from various disciplinary and legal risks.

PART 3: FINALLY

14. SOME FINAL THOUGHTS

As this book shows, Compliance can and often does play a huge range of roles within a modern organisation: adviser, checker, police officer (or at least security guard), drafter and reviewer of procedures. Compliance performs a key role in the organisation's controls. At the same time, Compliance must stay firmly grounded within the organisation. It has to keep its eyes and ears open.

Compliance also has to communicate. It has to tell, explain and interpret to people within the entity what it or the rules require. It has to report to the Board on what is going on and the regulatory problems that the organisation is likely to have to confront. It may have to speak to regulators once something has actually happened or is about to occur. Judging what to say and when and the choice of the right tone of friendliness, command, counsel or contrition – all the product of the personal attributes required of compliance people – could affect the future of organisations and many of those who work in them.

ABOUT ADAM SAMUEL

"Adam will tell anyone the right answer, regardless of who they are" was how one of the financial services industry's greats once described Adam to a bemused woman from a consumer organisation. He has devoted much of the last thirty-three years to trying to persuade almost every branch of the retail financial services industry to help itself and so treat its customers more fairly. Deliberately, under the radar, he has nursed, cajoled, provided the intellectual ammunition to and just supported people who wanted to do the right thing.

Coming from a background of qualifications as an English barrister and New York attorney, Adam has always believed that you cannot comfortably criticise people's professionalism unless you are as well-qualified as them. To this end, he has held qualifications as a financial and mortgage adviser for many years as well as the Chartered Institute of Securities and Investments (CISI) Compliance Diploma. He is, though, probably prouder of his St John's Ambulance Certificate in First Aid.

In the compliance area, Adam has worked with almost every corner of the retail scene from the major banks, building societies, insurers, financial advisers and mortgage intermediaries to tiny firms. Lawyers have used him both as a sounding board and as an expert witness. He has trained, lectured to and advised firms and trade bodies in the UK, Cyprus and Hong Kong. Adam has also written two books on complaint handling, a large part of a major practitioner looseleaf publication on regulation and regular articles for a number of publications, including a twenty-year column for *Compliance Monitor*.

You can contact Adam through his website: adamsamuel.com

OTHER BOOKS BY ADAM SAMUEL

Jurisdictional Problems in International Commercial Arbitration - A Study of Belgian, Dutch, English, French, Swedish, Swiss, US and West German Law, Schulthess, Zurich 1989, 333 pages

Consumer Complaints and Compensation: A Guide to the Financial Services Market, City and Financial, London 2005, 638 pages

Consumer Financial Services Complaints and Compensation, Thomson Reuters, London 2017, 909 pages

Printed in Great Britain
by Amazon

37970495R00066